AN ISRAELI AT THE COURT OF ST. JAMES'S

An Israeli at the Court of St. James's

Hanoch Bartov

Translated from the Hebrew by Ruth Aronson

VALLENTINE, MITCHELL—LONDON

First published in Hebrew
in Israel 1969.

First published in Great Britain 1971
by Vallentine, Mitchell & Co. Ltd.,
18 Cursitor Street, London, E.C.4.

Copyright © 1969 Hanoch Bartov

English Translation © 1971
Vallentine, Mitchell & Co. Ltd.

ISBN 0 853 03137 1

All rights reserved. No part of this publication may be reproduced, stored in a retrieval system, or transmitted, in any form or by means, electronic, mechanical, photocopying recording or otherwise without the prior permission in writing of
Vallentine, Mitchell & Co. Ltd.

Printed and bound by The Garden City
Press Ltd., Letchworth, Hertfordshire.

CONTENTS

THE NORMAN, THE MANDATE— AND THE COURT OF ST. JAMES'S	1
LEARNING TO MOVE, DRESS, EAT AND BEHAVE	8
LUNCH AT THE ATHENAEUM	20
THE ESTABLISHMENT: WHO IS AND WHO IS NOT	27
LONDON BRIDGE IS COMING DOWN	38
THE CELTIC LEAGUE AND ELIEZER BEN YEHUDA	51
HER MAJESTY'S SOCIALIST GOVERNMENT	55
KING ARTHUR'S LAND'S END	71
FAR FROM WHITECHAPEL, FAR FROM JERUSALEM	90
THE JEWS OF MAY AND JUNE	111
ON ONE INTELLECTUAL AND ON ANOTHER	135
TO: THE READER FROM: THE AUTHOR	144

THE NORMANS, THE MANDATE—
AND THE COURT OF ST. JAMES'S

IT WAS A full nine-hundred years after William the Norman vanquished Harold the Englishman at Hastings that we made our landing, come in peace, at Heathrow Airport. We were aware then as now that, since that one notorious Norman invasion, all efforts on the part of sundry foreigners to take possession of this green and pleasant isle have crashed upon the white cliffs of Dover. We were aware, too, that Britishers continue to regard any outsider with some suspicion. Small wonder that it was the English who invented radar: the nose of every Englishman seems to come equipped with a tiny built-in detecting device which helps him to tell a foreigner at first sound. Just to help matters, we never missed a chance to announce our origin, nor would we ever fail to mention that we were emissaries of a Foreign Power, here for just a while. This done, and being—in so far as possible—who and what we are, we felt fine. Or perhaps I should disclose right now, at the very outset, that we actually fell rather in love with the island and its people.

Not only England, said André Maurois, every Englishman is an island. And the truth of it seems to be that to break one's way through to the island's inhabitants is hardly less of a feat than to conquer the island itself. Nowadays, people the world over are constantly on the go: millions swarm, summer after summer, to the lands of the other millions. In the past, namely, Yesterday, this island was insulated against the outside world. Here they lived for centuries, the British, with lots of water all around, never missing those foreigners encamped somewhere across the Channel. Once, so goes the story, a fierce storm was raging in the Channel and all vessels were forced to seek harbour.

The B.B.C.'s version of the episode was that the Continent was cut off. Today, or so we are told, all that is gone; ours is a single world, its cities throng with foreigners of every people, race and kind—all together in the same, ever more international mixed bag. Yet even today one finds that something which took nine hundred years to make does not vanish overnight. Besides, England has a rather unusual quality: one cannot realistically hope to conquer her, but one can easily become captive to her uniqueness.

That is what happened to other Israelis, and it happened to us, too. Bear in mind, first and foremost, that the British Mandate over Palestine entitled us to a kind of mandate over Britain. As children, we learned the Britishers' language out of New Method Readers, as written and illustrated for distant India, and we would recite 'Once there was a wizard.' We used to have all kinds of Englishmen —High Commissioners, Secretary-Generals, District Commissioners and District Officers, as well as plain English coppers. Far away, in London, there was a Colonial Office, and the leaders of the Jewish Agency and our National Committee used to argue issues with it, to enter into conflict with it, to hope for salvation, to despair, to travel back and forth. Was it not the White Paper of Malcolm Macdonald, the then Colonial Secretary, against which we demonstrated? And then the whole business of illegal immigration: who was all the fuss about if not that villain of a Bevin, in whose honour we renamed the militarised zone in the centre of Jerusalem 'Bevingrad'? On the other hand, who could forget the many Righteous Gentiles, whose names alone would thrill us to the marrow—Lord Balfour, Wedgwood, Strabolgi? And Tel Aviv's 'General Allenby Street'? And Jerusalem's 'King George V Street'? And all that poetry we had to learn by heart for our matriculation: 'If Winter comes, can Spring be far behind?'

The Mother of Colonies is, of course, Petah Tikva— my hometown. Yet from another point of view, did not London play that role for my generation of Israelis? The sun never set in the Empire, and on the map half the world was coloured red, and no navy came anywhere near the Royal Navy. Shirley Temple was uppermost in the minds of amiable colonial colonels. The leaders of Palestine Jewry could be seen marching at the funeral of George V, or was it the coronation of George VI? The British were always very present in our minds.

But when we landed at Heathrow Airport all that—and much more—was in the distant past. Not only the Battle of Hastings, nine hundred years before almost to the day; not only the passing of Shakespeare, three hundred and fifty; the Great Fire of London, three hundred. All the big things had already happened: Trafalgar and Waterloo, the founding and ending of the British Raj in India, the start and finish of our own Mandate. The characters 'Ind. Imp.' no longer appeared on the penny. The Beatles were England's national heroes. And the real ruler of Great Britain was Harold the Second, who just a few months before our arrival had won an impressive majority in Parliament and had again taken over as Prime Minister of Her Majesty's Socialist Government.

The skies of France were clear and summery, but the Channel remained draped in a heavy curtain of cloud. Only occasionally could we catch a glimpse of the chequered patches of green far below. Just as we were about to land, however, the clouds drew apart for a while, and we had our first sight of the megalopolis: here endless rows and rows of single or double-storied brick houses of brown and black and grey, there the rich green of fields and hedges, gracious manors and little farmhouses, woods and copses, soft hills beneath a pale, sunless sky—as if all the colours had washed into the fine drizzle (oh, yes, it was raining all right), dripping into one another, the shade merging into the light, the sky into the earth, the green (of parks big and small, of sportsfields and commons) into the winding maze of the city's streets, in among the thousands upon thousands of buildings in which eight million people live and work—let alone the endless miles of suburbs which, in point of fact, are the city, which live off it and which house another four million or so of its breadwinners and its eggs-and-bacon eaters.

We landed in the thin drizzle, at Europe's biggest airport. They have not even finished constructing it, and it is already overcrowded. It simply does not have room for all the people who pass through it on their way to and from every corner of the globe. It is all concrete, glass, chromium and electronics, and an intoxicating international buzz. A strange sensation (even after all these years of Statehood), and a fact I make a mental note of, the special treatment accorded my diplomatic passport. I wish you a pleasant stay, Sir. Thank you, Sir.

The motorway bisects the rural landscape brutally, cutting through trees, sheep, fenced-in fields, angular stone churches, Constable-like canvases, pre-industrial England. But here is the road itself, set up on high concrete pillars, rising above the rows of London houses all so alike, elbow to elbow, built of bricks that seem to have been laid in some dark grey coffee-coloured mess. Just above us, on top of our car, rests the sky, a woolly grey water-sodden blanket. Everyone seems to be travelling in the wrong direction, and we keep our eyes glued anxiously to the wheel, expecting an accident. On that and other occasions, travelling on a mammoth double-decker, I make another mental note: I am struck by the patient, forbearing manner of the drivers as they make their way along the winding roads, never veering from the left-hand side, never hooting, neither going through red lights nor failing to stop at a pedestrian crossing or when some other car has the right of way. I feel like doing something about it. How can they possibly expect to get anywhere if they stick to traffic regulations that way, if they turn left when you'd expect them to turn right, calmly crawling along a mess of streets which are all absolutely identical. Another mental note: the passengers are no less sanguine than the drivers, sitting there with their mouths tightly clamped, calmly indifferent to their fate, the mystery of this labyrinth an open book to them.

These are the first moments, the first riddles we try to solve. All the streets, houses, signposts that keep coming inexorably towards us are identical. How does a person know if he is coming or going? Where is north? And the sun, for instance, where does it rise and where set—if at all, unless it, too, has dissolved into the sodden mess of sky? And the stars, are there stars in the London heavens, or does that blanket simply reflect the reddish glimmer of millions of windows, street-lamps, neon-lights, furnaces, cars, trains?

And here we stop, at the entrance to a gloomy-looking building of copper-coloured stone with ornamental domes, arched windows, columns, and a liveried doorman in front —an edifice as bloated as those who built it, across the road from a place we seem to have known all our lives, Hyde Park. This is our hotel, and the street is Bayswater, also an old friend. Did not the house of Forsyte rise and fall in these environs? And Kensington, the other park we can see from the window of our room—is it not the backyard of that romantic pair, the Princess and the Photographer? Then, looking the other way (what would it be, east?) between our window and Marble Arch, could we not see a host of Gates so heavy with history that even a Samson would be crushed beneath their weight—Lancaster, Marlborough, Clarendon, Stanhope and all the rest? And not the gates alone, but the stately houses, too. O England, whose history one seems to have absorbed like some favourite family conversation-piece, here you are in front of us, hidden in the rain, from those beheaded in the Tower to the last of the great, who died of old age in his Hyde Park home, the man who—so ironically—said that he had not been made His Majesty's Prime Minister in order to liquidate the Empire....

Well, so much for our Edwardian hotel and our first taste of English history. Alas, we had barely got our bags unpacked when a colleague of mine muttered something about being careful after dark, and keeping an eye on our over-curious youngsters. 'The neighbourhood isn't what it used to be. Bayswater, Queensway, to say nothing of Notting Hill Gate are rather ... how shall I put it? They've turned a lot of the town houses into tenements, chock-full of questionable types. I don't want you to get the wrong idea,' says our colleague helpfully, 'but the area does have rather a lot of prostitutes, addicts, migrants, gaolbirds. No, no,' adds our colleague hastily, 'your hotel is first-rate, we got you rooms here on purpose. After all, your window faces one of the loveliest, and most exclusive parts of the city. There's Embassy Row and Palace Green—that's where we have our Embassy—and the Park itself, of course. Then there's Knightsbridge across the way, and Mayfair just over there—all very upper-class. Point is, I just thought you might like to get your bearings....'

We take in every word, but we do not get our bearings. Each fresh piece of information merely adds to our confusion. So we make a resolution : we'll take our time, look around slowly, try and impose some order on the flood of new impressions, we shall muster some British patience. Things will sort themselves out eventually. We reminded ourselves of an earlier venture, our trip to the United States. Now, as then, we had two whole years ahead of us, so we resolved to employ the same technique again—let things happen.

It was an excellent resolution, which took two full years to implement. Shall I divulge a further secret ? When we took our leave, to go back home, we discovered that most of the riddles had remained unsolved, most of the puzzles as bewildering as ever. How could we have expected it to be otherwise ?

One further word. The author of these lines had some years earlier written a light comedy—*Our Founding Father* —on the theme of Israeli diplomats and the Israeli image abroad. Fate played a joke on me and made me, too, into a diplomat: on the staff of our Ambassador to the Court of St. James's, as protocol has it. When I arrived in England, a fellow-diplomat asked me whether the Minister had seen my play. I replied that I neither knew nor cared, but I did not bother to enquire why he was asking. Now I realise that my diplomatic status has not turned me into the hero of a major drama ; I only hope it has not fitted me for a role in some minor comedy, either. I was offered all kinds of advice before embarking on my mission. The best was that given me by someone I now recognise as very wise. He said: 'Don't make an effort to look like a diplomat. Act as if you are—what you are.' And that I tried very hard to do.

My diplomatic status is relevant only because it afforded me a superb opportunity for meeting all kinds of people. It meant I could circulate in both the drawing-rooms and the engine-rooms of English society, it enabled me to peep now and then into the corridors of power in this country and—what I naturally found most interesting of all

—get to know its Jewish community. It was not a premeditated crime. It just happened, as a bye-product of the job I chanced to have. In addition to tax-free whisky and tobacco, this was the real diplomatic privilege I enjoyed.

There is a catch to all good things, of course. There is a price one has to pay for such privileges. It was not merely the fact that for two long years I could not get out of my respectable dark suit or that, when on duty, I turned into the epitome of the perfect gentleman. What I refer to is a restriction which a friend of mine who had worked as a censor during the Mandate once described as follows. Material that goes through your hands can be classified in four ways: the bulk is neither secret nor of any interest; some of it is confidential, but that does not mean it is not dull; some makes fascinating reading but it's not for telling; and the fourth category consists of stuff that one can and wants to talk about. The characterisation of my censor-friend guided me in setting down what follows in the pages below.

LEARNING TO MOVE, DRESS, EAT AND BEHAVE

THE FIRST piece of advice for anybody coming to London is: never leave your hotel unless equipped with the travellers' Guide to the Perplexed, that greatest of all best-sellers, modestly entitled *A to Z*. A sizeable pocket-book, it has a street-map of the metropolis spread over the first 128 pages, all in close-cramped lines and microscopic print. The last 137 pages consist entirely of an index of some twenty-eight thousand streets, give or take a few thousand. It's not hard to visualise the Odyssey that awaits our hero.

The main difficulty is not the horrendous number of streets, it's their peculiar logic, bound to bewilder even the most sophisticated of foreigners. Ordinarily, you don't expect to find two streets with the same name in the same place. Take the Americans, for instance, whom we all tend to patronise. Well, they like to number their streets, either from A to Z or from one to infinity. Theirs might be a slightly impersonal kind of system, but it's enormously helpful. You land in Manhattan with an address in hand—all you need to do is find it: uptown, downtown, East Side or West Side. The houses are numbered with the selfsame logic, what's more. All nice and straightforward.

Not so London. Here's what happened to us during our first few weeks there, by way of illustration. At the time, we were desperately trying to find a place to live and looking up our first few contacts. Someone would tell you, in a vague sort of manner: ' Oh, yes, that will be on Kensington . . . (there follows an indistinct mumble, lost in a blur of words which you don't ask him to repeat as you don't want to sound provincial and, besides, you *know* what the man meant) . . . you just can't miss it.' Being an Israeli, and a seasoned traveller, you exude an air of total self-assurance, as though you had been told it was off Dizengoff, which would mean *the* street of Tel-Aviv. So you find a street which fits the description, you even track down the right number after a relatively brief search. Alas, it is not the one you were after. So you go up to the first person in sight and, if he isn't one of those blasted foreigners that are inundating London these days, he will quite literally go out of his way to help you. You can rest assured that he will not let go of you unless and until he has explained in the utmost detail, not once but thrice, how to reach your destination. He will even accompany you part of the way, and is sure not to take leave of you without declaring quite emphatically: 'You just can't miss it.'

He will, however, begin by trying to clear up a minor problem. 'Kensington Street, you say? Are you quite sure, sir, that they said "street"?' By this time you have lost some of your confidence, you're beginning to get a little rattled, and so you reply with a question of your own: 'If not street, what then?' 'Oh,' your Londoner will give a mischievous smile, 'we have any number of roads named Kensington around here in the borough of Kensington. There's Kensington High Street, and then there is Church Street, and Road, and a small court in the middle of a huge block called Kensington Court. Or could it be Kensington Palace Gardens that you're after?'

How should I know?

Yet that is the simplest kind of predicament. In a case like that you can at least assume (though you still need to watch your step) that all the said streets are within a single borough and hence more or less in the same vicinity. The city we now know as London is in fact a conglomerate of dozens of towns and villages which used to be miles from the City of London, which used to be miles from the City of Westminster. Each had its own High Street and Broadway, its Church Street and King's Road, its Market Street and The Green. People never concerned themselves with the other places in those days. When they all joined to become part of London, the streets kept their old names. At best, they simply tacked on the name of the borough. There are any number of London Roads and King's Roads and Park Roads in the London of today. How on earth am I supposed to know which exactly is the one I need.... ?

I did eventually learn that one should never dare step out of the hotel without first writing down the precise name of the street and part of the city one wants to get to, and that one must always include the tricky little cipher meant to indicate that W.12 is nowhere near W.1. Yet even after one has taken every possible precaution, the wayfarer's prayer is still in order. Do not expect to find a number on each house; a large building or court is quite likely to make do with no more than a mere Christian name. The logic is peculiar, but very English: it stands to reason that if you are someone who ought to know, you will; if you don't, proof enough you shouldn't, so please don't be a nuisance.

Say the house does have a number, and you have managed to find the proper street, you may still have a surprise in store. You may discover that the street isn't numbered in the normal way, with odd numbers going up one side and even numbers the other, but that they go from one to such-and-such on this side and from such-and-such up on the other, or that they follow some other ingenious design sure to confound the foreigner.

I love to brag about my excellent sense of direction. London defeated me. I would get into my car at A, with the clearly-mapped intention of reaching B. I'd follow the winding streets, never losing my sense of purpose or direction, though forced every now and then to yield to the city's vagaries. Suddenly, God knows when or how, I would take a wrong turning and find myself completely lost. I never knew whether I was getting nearer to or further from my destination. I used to liken those early drives in London to the throwing of a boomerang: you send yourself off into space and end up back precisely where you started.

Very well, then, how did I avoid getting permanently lost?

That brings us to the moral of our tale. One day, after we had been in London for four or five months or so, I suddenly discovered that I was able both to begin *and* end a journey. I would be given an address and would know its whereabouts, even which parts of the city I should be crossing on my way, even whether it lay east or west. Please do not ask me how that miracle was wrought. One does not question miracles.

And it was then that I made another, even more significant, discovery. As I kept losing my way and blundering about in its endless maze, the city somehow began to emerge for me; the beauty of London tucked away behind the disarray of houses glued together, winding in and out along its winding streets, sprawled out in its eternal drizzle, began to make a kind of sense. The total lack of a well-ordered system or logic which is London forms a harmony of its own, complex and fascinating. So numerous are its impressive edifices that a long, long time must pass before one can thrill to the discovery of a particular façade, a familiar curve of the Thames, a certain pub. Only then can one begin to conceive the sum-total of what millions have constructed here in the course of many generations, from the labyrinthine docks in the east to the City, commercial pulse of London; the political heart of the Empire, stretched out between St. Paul's and Westminster, Trafalgar Square, Buckingham Palace and Hyde Park. One gradually comes to recognise the styles of the different eras, in Knightsbridge, Regent's Park, Hampstead—an architectural Tower of Babel which makes it easier to understand the principles underlying Britain's social system. Just as Britain has no written Constitution, but an intricate network of Acts, Precedents, Usages and Traditions, so nothing works here in accordance with some preconceived and detailed master-plan forced upon it from an omniscient central authority. A master-plan of this kind was once devised following the Great Fire, but the English—stiff-necked and jealous guardians of their own eccentric egos—managed to outwit that as well. Yet again, with all the British objection to conformity, with everybody endeavouring to be out of step, as it were, the sum-total of all these eccentricities is more harmonious than any master-plan, and not one whit less English than the familiar stock-types of anecdotes and satire.

In short, I learned to move, and I learned what I was moving through, and that one needs to exercise both caution and perseverance in order not to lose one's way among the many corridors en route. Fifty generations of Englishmen are reflected in the fleeting image of the present generation, itself in turn but the first of fifty more. Who would argue that all this should arrange itself to suit the temporary needs of a guest?

There were several other things we learned in those initial months: how to dress, eat, talk and behave.

Before embarking on our mission we had been carefully briefed on what a man should wear and how a woman must dress lest the name of Israel be besmirched among the Gentiles. We took careful note of all such information, and made two resolutions: the first—never to violate Protocol; the second—to put off implementing the first until such time as we could see for ourselves how they dress, those Englishmen we were supposed to try and dress like.

They say that things are not what they used to be. The young people in bizarre Carnaby Street get-ups, the girls in mini-skirts, the foreigners pouring in from all kinds of god-forsaken places, the breaking down of class barriers— all these have supposedly affected the pedantically formal conservatism of English dress. That may well be true. We could see for ourselves that things were not the same as when we visited London in the early 'fifties. We need not invariably don a hat, gloves and inoffensive suit when we ventured out. London women—young and not so young alike, and that includes typists and shopgirls as well— seemed to dress with a daring abandon which was all the more striking when contrasted with the decline of fashion in Paris. The balance had changed between the two cities. King's Road was now the *dernier cri*. There was something of the same mood in the informal way men dressed, even on traditionally formal occasions: tieless at the theatre, hatless in the Foreign Office, lounge suits in the Buckingham Palace Gardens.

No need to overstate the point. Nothing is more uniformly colourfully black than the gentlemen who throng

London Bridge, all in dark suits, all in bowler hats, all with umbrellas folded, hurrying to work in the City. And then there are the gentlemen in their invariable salt-and-peppers, or the ones who stick to a striped, double-breasted, loose and baggy, never-new suit. And of course the uniforms—of chauffeurs, porters, transport workers, let alone liveried butlers and waiters in full attire. The many variations of the sartorial establishment—some quite obvious, others so subtle as to be discernible only to the experienced eye—can be most unnerving to a foreigner coming from a country where many still take care not to appear well dressed. Such nuances of dress, moreover, are not confined merely to the traditionally conservative sections of British society. The non-conformists seem to have equally strict codes all of their own. The intellectuals and artists in corduroys and flannel shirts, knitted ties and hush-puppies, appear to conform to a code no less rigorous than that of the Carnaby Street set. People dress to suit their class and calling, the social and business circles in which they move; to comply with their image of themselves and of what society expects them to look like. To dress is to conform, to dress is to rebel. A working-man from the East End is always recognisable, even in his Sunday best. Or take the unforgettable sight of hundreds of young and not so young middle-class matrons assembled on a bright spring morning for some affair not far from the Prince Albert Memorial—they will all be wearing bright print frocks and coats, flowery hats and neat pastel gloves, festooned with jewellery; each and every one her own individual self, yet all of them together having the look of a regiment decked out for the Commanding Matron's Parade.

    The rules are highly intricate and inexorable. There is no law to enforce them, but then no one would ever dream of breaking them. You wear this on week-days and that on week-ends. You know in advance what to wear to dinner: it's formal, semi-formal or informal. There's a world of difference between a black-tie and a white-tie affair, and the Lord have mercy on the poor chap who gets all togged-up for a day in the country. You can hardly address a prayer to the Almighty in one of London's posher synagogues without dressing up first, and it is hard to imagine a real wedding without a morning-coat. Being a diplomat—albeit as unorthodox and lowly as the present writer—was doubly taxing because it was not only his own personal standing that was at stake but that of his country, too.

We tried our best to master the rules, and took grateful note of every tip from friends or colleagues. We got to know that a true gentleman will at the very least wear ready-mades labelled Simpson or Austin Reed, and that he will bow to the law of *noblesse oblige* by fitting out a wardrobe to meet all and any sartorial eventuality. Ourselves succumbing to the call of duty, we first began to yawn and then to ruffle through our pockets worriedly.

Then one day I had the good fortune to overhear someone saying that the Prime Minister sported Burton suits. Well, said I, if that's the case, why don't I do just that and forget the rest. After all, if the occasion demands a white tie, there is always Moss Bros. to run to. So I stocked in a supply of suits and shirts to give myself that sense of security which suits and shirts seemed to give everybody else, and decided that I was ready to win friends and influence people.

At that point we were prepared to entertain and be entertained. Here, too, we faced a far from undemanding enterprise. I shall merely mention a few of the secrets of the game as they unfolded for us through a painful process of trial and error. The crux of the whole business is the rigmarole which precedes and concludes every such affair: sending out the invitations, and the R.S.V.P.s that follow, in the same politely-worded clichés, and then the thank-you notes (the guest's wife to the host's wife, of course). Of all the varied forms of hospitality, we found an invitation to dinner the most rewarding. You are asked to come at 7.30 p.m. for 8.00, and you find to your embarrassment that this does not mean that you can turn up at 8.30, say. Somehow everybody always managed to be there right on time, no matter what, the company will always have a sherry, will always beat about the bush noiselessly and at length as if it were the real thing, until on the dot of eight comes the magic word—and dinner is served. There are certain touches—a French cook, a butler, a more formal brand of informality—which set a dinner at one of the large town houses in Kensington, Holland Park or Mayfair apart from its counterpart in the more bohemian setting of Hampstead, Greenwich or Chelsea; but they're all the same basically. Dinner may be served in the lounge or in a separate dining-room, names may be printed on cards or the guests seated by the host; it is always a meticulously pre-planned operation. This is the moment of truth. First consider the golden rule of never having couples sit next to one another, of always having men and women alternate around the table, and then you discover the relative status of the guests by the men's relative proximity to the hostess and the women's to the host. A most delicate and complicated art.

Next comes the food, and again you are faced with the question of what and how. We can dismiss the what; suffice to say that at times we were victims of some rather dreadful English cooking, at others we sampled some of what the righteous must be served in paradise. Our problem was the how. We employed a simple technique: we would peek at our neighbours and then ape them shamelessly—use the silver they used, eat the way they ate, drink as they did, stop when they did, smile their smiles, talk their talk. Hard work—but we are used to hardships. If my memory serves me right, it was George Brown who declared, when appointed Foreign Secretary, that his not eating fish with two different forks was hardly likely to imperil Britain's foreign policy. We dared not take such risks, but it cost us a good deal in effort and in loss of appetite. A further ordeal was being obliged to keep a conversation going, and scintillating, to both left and right of us. The going would get really rough when we happened to be in the company of that uniquely English type of conversationalist whose lip-less, voiceless mumble we were quite unable to decipher. Yet more frustrating was their tendency to load their talk with pauses, bridging the gap between one word and the next by a slight change of intonation or an enigmatic hmmm.

That was for the first little while. In the end I grew accustomed to the mumbling and the cutlery, and it was all very pleasant. Just one more comment on this subject. I once read that that man-about-town par excellence, Henry James, who was a regular and welcome denizen of all the fashionable salons of his day, had achieved the quite remarkable record of one hundred dinner parties in the space of a single year. Only now am I in a position to appreciate the magnitude of that accomplishment. Well, if Henry James could be acclaimed for a feat of that kind, I—who was brought up rather differently in my mother's parlour in dear little old Petah Tikva—should be doubly acclaimed.

Well, then. Having got through the dessert without mishap, all wait for the hostess to rise and ask the ladies if they wish to powder their noses. They all wish to, and follow her out of the dining-room. The men stay behind for a brandy and cigar, both excellent for the digestion and for masculine conversation. After the proper interval, the host will mutely query (yes, I really heard it many times): 'Shall we join the ladies?' I do not recall a case where some gentleman declined. Once again the conversation glows in a bright heterosexual flame. Everyone has coffee, possibly another drink. Then, ten times out of ten, one of the men will give a startled look at his watch and mutter, 'Good heavens. Almost eleven-thirty. Hate to break up this lovely party, but we really must be getting along.' Whereupon everyone gets up, just as surprised and just as in a hurry. The following day, all the ladies will be penning handwritten notes on light blue stationery—how delicious the food was, what an interesting group of people the guests were, thank you so much for such a pleasantly memorable evening.

And that was how we learned to eat and to behave.

I found myself talking endlessly. In the London we inhabited, talk was the price one had to pay for a substantial dinner. Sometimes, however, the food was merely an excuse for substantial talking. I once knew a globe-trotting Israeli VIP who, whenever he would get back home, would assure me that it had not been all fun—those dinners are murder, he'd say. I would sort of smirk, and he would feel offended: 'You may laugh, but they *are* a burden.' Now that I have had to carry the same cross myself, I tend to agree. The difficulty is not in the eating, but in the talking. The American, like the Israeli, talks in a loud and definite tone of voice; his statements are short and readily interpreted, rather like a television commercial. To an Englishman, however, nothing is more abhorrent than the direct, conclusive, unqualified statement. In order to join in a conversation in a semi-intelligent fashion, I had to train my ear to listen, and I had to learn to follow and grasp what was being said. A person will never cut you short, Israeli style, with an outright 'Sorry, but you're talking rubbish!' Instead he will mutter something to the effect of: 'Yes . . . Yes . . . You have a point there. Most interesting. . . . I'd like to give it some more thought, mhmm, just now it's not quite clear precisely. . . .' He will not resort to the straightforward path of simply telling you that his own views are diametrically opposed to yours. Rather, he will start out with a hesitant stammer and then go on to say something tentative, like: 'Well, yes, of course . . . but wouldn't you be inclined to agree that one might look at things from a rather different angle. I mean, er, well of course you may be quite right in what you say, but I would say that X's view of the matter does seem to merit some consideration. You see, he does tend to point out a not uninteresting further point which just might conceivably change the balance of . . . etc.'

At all events, that was how we almost unwittingly learned to talk. An Israeli conversation is not unlike a Greek chorus—everyone talks at the same time. The only difference is that each individual voices his own private text, and when the other voices seem to interfere, he simply raises his own. The English, on the other hand, believe that the art of civilised conversation lies not so much in the tongue as in the ear. How would I know that what I was saying was falling on deaf ears? When the person I was addressing would start giving a series of recurrent and somnolent nods, accompanied by a murmured 'Yes . . . Yes . . . Yes . . .'

To cut a long story short: the dark suit settled one problem, and we eliminated the next obstacle by adopting the set rules and regulations of approved social conduct. Strict compliance with what is regarded as good manners—compulsive punctuality, a prompt reply to every letter and, most important, saying 'Thank you' as often as possible including in response to the 'Thank you' of another—saved us a lot of trouble. Now that I come to think of it, it was even very pleasant.

At this point we were ready to start concentrating on what we were here for. We did our utmost to go places, meet people, observe and listen. I remember a charming old lady who came over to me at one of our invariable receptions. 'I've been having an argument with some acquaintances,' she confessed. 'They insist that every Embassy has several people involved in espionage. Well, I told them that I was not prepared to swear for any of the others, but that I was and am utterly convinced that the Israelis would never go in for anything so dreadful.' As she spoke, I was reminded of what a friend had said to me recently, only half in jest: 'They say you're the only Cultural Attaché who's seriously attached to culture.' Now it suddenly dawned on me that they were both wrong: it was *I* who was the real spy.

Let me put it this way. All those afternoons and evenings, all those people—including some who were to become very dear friends—all my activities—including some which I undertook with a deep sense of purpose—failed to drive out a certain imp that had taken possession of the control-centre of my brain, where he did the most outrageous things. He was totally uninvolved, just sat there watching and taking notes in his private spy-code. In fact, spying became so much of a habit with him, that just as he would spy on everything I saw or heard, so he would not hesitate to spy on *me*. Sometimes, at my most solemn moments, he would lose control and burst out with a weird laugh audible to none but me, ringing at the back of my head. He caused me no end of trouble, that fellow, and now is my chance to get even with him. Once I caught him unawares, and snatched his coded corpus from him. Now as I try to set down my impressions of what we saw and heard, I do not rely on my own memory alone, but help myself liberally to the rascal's notes. May the good Lord forgive me, and may all my good friends, too. The latter should take comfort from the fact that the one to use the notes is not *he*, heaven forbid, but *I*. And I can lay claim to at least one virtue—being a diplomat. Retired.

LUNCH AT THE ATHENAEUM

I WAS STILL in the process of adjusting my old self to my new circumstances, when I was asked by the director of a world-famous art gallery to have lunch with him at his club, the Athenaeum.

No use denying it: I was so excited that I could hardly wait for the moment when I would—at long last—set foot inside the portals of that holy of holies, that bastion of the Establishment, so celebrated in literature and legend. Having already learned from bitter experience that no crime was more heinous than not being on time, I took every precaution to arrive several minutes before the appointed hour, which was 12.45 p.m.

So there I was, standing in Waterloo Place face to face with a Greek-templish façade with pillars and all, painted in an inimitable yellow with the helmeted figure of Athene, goddess of wisdom and warfare, in bold plastered relief atop the pillars. Associations go all the way back to Classical Greece, which is what the founders of the club must also have had in mind. But history did not stop at Waterloo. To my right stretches Lower Regent Street, with its massively gloomy buildings symbolic of a power hard as stone. To my left are gracious patrician mansions, material evidence of former times, never to return. Immobile in the Place are the heroes of Waterloo, India and the Crimea, generals and ministers of the Crown, now ancient history themselves.

Restlessly my eye wanders from my watch to the broad flights of stairs leading down to the road which has borne many a Royal Parade, from the gates of Buckingham Palace running along St. James's Park and on to Admiralty Arch and Whitehall—or was it the other way around? If only the sun does not betray them, thousands of clerks and typists from the offices around will soon be swarming into the park, coming from Whitehall or across the Mall to bask in the precious sun.

This is the place, this is the time—12.42 in front of the Athenaeum. Will the reader kindly step into my shoes, see through my eyes, have his heart beat as rapidly as mine? Taxi-cabs, government Humbers, Rolls-Royces of the mighty and the proud draw up in front of the yellowish building, chauffeurs hurry out to open the door for their occupants (the former all in the navy-blue uniform of their calling, the latter in dark blues or browns or greys, bowler hats, furled umbrellas, nearly all middle-aged or more, the rest advancing, well-groomed, towards middle age), and then hurry back to the wheel to make room for more cars and more club-men. People walk up the stairs. So do I.

Inside the massive front-door to the left is an ancient booth. Ancient gentlemen—tall, starched and dignified—eye me from inside and from outside the booth. They are evidently not members of the House of Lords, so they must be on the staff of the club. *They* have no such doubts as to who I am, immediately sense that I do not belong to the place and inquire—very, very courteously I must say—whether they can help me, sir. I thereupon mention the—very, very distinguished I must say—name of my host, which is enough to make me feel as though I myself were knighted by the very sound of saying 'Sir So-and-So.' They thereupon examine their records to see whether he has in fact booked a table and whether he has arrived. Yes, sir, Sir So-and-So is expected but no, sir, Sir So-and-So has not yet arrived. Would you wish to dispose of your coat? (I had forgotten my newly-acquired hat on the train, and I do not carry an umbrella on principle.) Wash your hands? Have a look at the ticker?

The hour is 12.45 and there is no sign of my host. So I do all of the above. I spend a while in front of the tickers which keep typing out the latest news, all the news all the time, particularly the state of affairs on the stock exchange (which is of great importance) and (which is of even greater importance) at the horse-races. Apropos of gambling and betting, at which the English seem to be unrivalled, I am reminded that it was from the neighbouring Reform Club that a certain punctilious Englishman set out—to win a bet, no more, no less—on his Eighty Days Around the World.

Thinking of the Reform (where I was to lunch in due course in similarly distinguished company) sets me thinking about that peculiar English institution—the Club—which, believe it or not, exists not only in the Pickwick Papers but in real life, too. I look around and see members making their way up and down the broad staircase leading to the upper floor, see the bust of one of the Athenaeum's most noted members, Charles Darwin. Did not Charles Dickens, another roving clubman, quarrel with Thackeray in the Garrick and then make friends with him again on these very stairs (or so I remember reading somewhere)?

So this is it: huge nineteenth-century dimensions, simultaneously grandiose and shabby, the real men-only establishment. This is where the moneyed and the landed gentry used to meet at leisure, where politicians would spin out intrigues and writers yarns, where the idle rich would indulge in a choice meal, have a game of cards, reminisce about their younger days in the far-flung reaches of the Empire across the seven seas. This is the London version of 'tout Paris'. Didn't they say that Harold Macmillan used to run his Government as if it were a club on week-days, a country-house at the week-end?

But here, at 12.51, is my host, hurrying towards me brimming with apologies for his unfortunate and, alas, unavoidable delay. Six full minutes late. Shocking. With my kind permission, we forgo a glass of sherry and proceed directly to the spacious dining-room, full of tables large and small, including a long salad table, at which I throw discreet looks. We are ushered to a small table at the window. After consulting the menu, we (or rather, he) decide to start with melon (which, my host assures me with dry club humour, they won't manage to ruin even at this club and which might well come from Israel). He selects a wine, and then suggests that we take sole, again for the same very good reason. In the Athenaeum—he quotes an oft-quoted quip of another distinguished member—one is likely to find all the arts but one, gastronomy.

I recall that day very vividly, not only because it was my first such experience but also because of the man I was privileged to lunch with. He was not what one thinks of as a typical club man. A tall, handsome and much-travelled man, he was a superb conversationalist with the rare ability to make me feel, in a matter of minutes, as though I had been born and bred at the Athenaeum. Nonetheless, I could see that being a member was not something insignificant and that, even in present-day England, it carried status. I could see, then and on other occasions, the right people meeting their opposite numbers, whether directors, editors, vice-chancellors or senior executives—in short, the string-pullers of society. Food means very little: the main course is being there, rubbing shoulders, talking about things.

Talking, yes, but rather like dolphins, in tones that scarcely reach the ordinary human ear. On that first occasion we had a small table to ourselves, but in other clubs we found ourselves seated at long tables with a whole lot of strangers. It is a curious English tradition which I encountered at universities as well as at the renowned—forgive the vulgar term—restaurant of Simpson's.

I cannot resist recounting an incident in which I was unwillingly involved at Simpson's. I had heard a great deal about the place, but had never had occasion to eat there. A short time before I was due to leave London, a friend of mine insisted that we go there so that I could see it all for myself. I was suitably attired, but the friend, a well-known writer, turned up dressed like a Cossack in boots, a silk polo-necked shirt and sheepskin coat. At the door he was gently but firmly refused admission. That is, it was suggested to him that he retire to the manager's office, where he would be given a shirt and tie. My friend, a big man, protested, saying that he did not believe the manager's chest could match his manly proportions. As neither side was willing to give in, I quietly followed my friend to his club, the Garrick. I use the word 'his' reservedly, since he did own a club so that he could (so he said) set his own rules.

To go back to my lunch at the Athenaeum. We spooned chunks of Stilton on to biscuits to top off our sole and salad. We finished off the last drop of wine with the cheese, and thereby pronounced ourselves ready for the next stage of the proceedings. We left behind us a dining-hall full of men at lunch, their lips moving soundlessly as in a silent film, and ascended the broad staircase with its well-worn carpet to the library. Here we helped ourselves to a cup of coffee, and settled down to smoke a cigar. The deep, rather faded leather chairs engulfed various elderly gentlemen, puffing at cigars, leafing through magazines, whispering to one another. Just like in an English novel. Just like the nineteenth century. In just such a leather chair, one of the elder members of the club had breathed his last, gently, quietly; three full days went by before they noticed a difference between him and the other members—namely, that he had passed away.

The two of us sat there, eternity on our hands, sipping coffee, smoking, talking. And when good wine is coursing through your veins, and you are enveloped in the aroma of a large Havana, and your companion is an intelligent, sophisticated man with a dry and somewhat caustic English wit, then time stands still. It could well be the nineteenth century.

Until a quarter to three. On the dot. At that precise moment the two of us simultaneously glance at our watches, equally amazed at the speed with which those two fine hours have passed, equally disdainful of the vagaries of this gross world from which, unfortunately, neither of us is free to escape. We put on our coats, go our separate ways, are swallowed up in the din of the metropolis. The end of the 'sixties. The last third of the twentieth century.

This was one shrine, one of the holy of holies. In due course, I came to frequent Pall Mall and St. James's Street, to discover clubland. Just before one o'clock everybody swarms in, and just before three o'clock everybody swarms out. The keys of the kingdom have made a single turn.

Or have they? Truth to tell, things are no longer what

they used to be. The vintage clubmen are pre-World War II. One wonders if there will ever again be diaries like those written by Sir Harold Nicolson or 'Chips' Channon, the last of the Pickwicks. Time is money, not only in America. The retired colonial administrators, officers and merchants have gone with the Empire, wafted away by a new wind. The enormous, fully-staffed town-houses have given way to the commuting age. The class that would discuss at leisure anything but money is still the pearl of the Crown; but a new class of high-powered real-estate men, contractors, industrialists, technologists, chain-store tycoons, lawyers, labour leaders, show-business magnates and press lords seem to have taken over.

People seem to have acquired a taste for—good gracious! —fine food, mixed company, the hectic pace. Nowadays, when somebody suggests lunch at the Club, he may have in mind the Playboy, right there on Park Lane, with Bonnies, Clydes, the lot. A particularly successful film producer will take you—in his Rolls—to Isow's for kreplach soup and tcholent. A with-it director might escort you—in his chauffeured Humber—to the White Elephant. Top commercial television executives will suggest Prunier's for sea food or Fu Tong for Chinese dishes, while many a busy man will make do with a quick lunch not far from his desk, which may be quite a distance away from Pall Mall.

Inside the Athenaeum, one has a peculiar sensation, as though one has come, at long last, into physical contact with the Establishment, has actually seen the Holy of Holies—a place which the High Priest alone may enter, and then not only on the Day of Atonement. I came to learn that this is not the case. No longer is it the place where people who count decide on things which matter. It is not even easy to keep them going. It breaks my heart, but I see nothing but gloom.

The creamy yellowish façade, like the worn-out carpets, like the gentlemen sunk in the soft leather chairs, suddenly look rather pathetic, like left-overs of a world that is no more. Theirs is a dying world. However, and this we came to learn much later, it is a very slow and extremely stubborn death.

One wishes it would never happen. Yet even if the clubs all disappear one day, they will leave a living heritage behind: the lengthy lunch at an elegant restaurant. The food there will be tastier, the service better, the furniture more modern, the talk louder. But there one will never again meet the true clubman, all the time in the world on his hands, confident of being central to the scheme of things, talking wittily and volubly, someone to give a Boswell, a Dickens or a James something to write about. There won't be any retired general there tugging at his white moustache as he relives Khartoum in a dream. London has joined the twentieth-century rat race, and money is a dirty word only among those who lack it. I can see now that not only Karl Marx and Lord (Simon) Marks deserve some credit. So does Groucho Marx for having said that he was not going to pay good money to join a club that let in people like him.

THE ESTABLISHMENT:
WHO IS AND WHO IS NOT

THE WORD 'establishment'—both in the original English version as well as in its newly-born Hebrew equivalent, 'mimsad'—is not entirely at home in the company of older, more matter of fact and well-established items of the Israeli lexicon. It has something of the parvenu about it—in itself, of course, a contradiction in terms. Translated into images, the concept is perceived as ancient walls of stone, as kings and cardinals and conquerors, as all that is permanent and deeply-rooted, the backbone of a dinosaur.

We came equipped with some idea of the history of the word in the English language. We knew that Henry VIII had established an ecclesiastical system at the head of which he had placed—naturally enough—the monarch. We knew that the Establishment was first and foremost the State Church, with the Archbishops of Canterbury and York as well as four-and-twenty bishops sitting in the House of Lords, with all church appointments made by the King, albeit through his Prime Minister. We were aware, moreover—having read History at the university—that in due course the word had come to denote other established organisations such as the Army, the Civil Service and so on.

Very simple, in fact. Or it used to be simple, factual, devoid of any further connotation. It is only recently that the word has acquired a broader, more all-inclusive sense. Nowadays one will never hear it pronounced in a neutral tone like, say, 'sheep' or 'nebula.' There is always a shade of irony, not as though the speaker were simply using the right word for the appropriate phenomenon but as if he wished to manifest an attitude, to take sides, so to speak, all in one breath. The Establishment is everybody who is inside, or so say the outsiders. Oddly enough, although one would expect the majority to profess adherence to the former category, most of the people I encountered would utter the word 'establishment' in a tone clearly meant to indicate that it is somewhere else, that they were outside it, or that *it* was outside them—which in turn means 'inside.'

So who *is* the Establishment?

Naturally enough, we found ourselves wondering quite a bit about the whole thing. We knew that, by virtue of our official role, we were supposed to be moving mostly inside the Establishment, and in England one seems to stumble on it everywhere; yet I have never been introduced to the man who would say, quite simply and straightforwardly, 'I am a member of the Establishment.' There were those about whom we had no doubts at all; there were others who seemed to go out of their way to deny the fact they were and who yet left us with our doubts; and there were some who simply dismissed the whole matter as insignificant. What precisely did Richard Crossman have in mind when he said: 'All my life I have watched the gyrations of the British Establishment. They move like a flight of starlings. One turns, all turn'? Who are *they*, the ones that turn together? Are there any Englishmen who, by their very nature, watch the gyrations from the outside? Or does any starling move and turn with the flock? Are we perhaps now witnessing some new kind of latterday starlings, who herald a new social spring? Or is it possible that those curious birds of the 'fifties, sharp-beaked, individualistic and raucous, have in the meantime been transformed into the saintly swans of Buckingham and Canterbury?

One thought of *Look Back in Anger* which, we were told, shocked Britain no less than had the Gunpowder Plot some three centuries before—and for much the same reasons. Jimmy Porter, crude representative of the post-war lower-class, got up and spat out the harsh truth—about the hollowness of the Monarchy, the hypocrisy of the Church, the furthering of an Empire that had ceased to exist. His was an anti-Establishment manifesto, or so we were led to think. I remembered a book I had picked up in a New York bookstore in 1960—*Declaration*. It contained pieces by writers and critics such as Colin Wilson, John Osborne, Kenneth Tynan and Doris Lessing. Ensconced in London, I could not help thinking of what Osborne had to say there:

'People are too bored by parsons to laugh at them any more. It is well known that often the funniest thing a comic can do is not do it, but the Church has overworked this moral gag . . . . People turned to other acts that could at least be relied upon to give the advertised performance. James Dean and Marilyn Monroe did good business. They were obviously genuine, they worked: you got your money's worth, they could be imitated. Was there an English act that could top the bill, that could be relied on to fill all sections of the house ? There was—it wasn't a very new act, but it was well organised, and completely brought up to date; that fabulous family we all love so well—the Amazing Windsors !

'My objection to the Royalty symbol is that it is dead ; it is the gold filling in a mouthful of decay. . . . When the mobs rush forward in The Mall they are taking part in the last circus of a civilisation that has lost faith in itself, and sold itself for a splendid triviality, for " the beauty of the ceremonial " and the " essential spirituality of the rite." We may not create any beauty or exercise much spirituality, but by God ! we've got the finest ceremonial and rites in the world ! Even the Americans haven't got that. . . .'

The book is packed with such and other heresies. For reasons I won't disclose for the time being, I shall cite one more extract here, this time from Kenneth Tynan's 'long ironic letter written to a young man . . . who was coming to the end of his three years at Oxford':

'Do I speak for you when I ask for a society where people care more for what you have learned than for where you learned it; where people who think and people who work can share common assumptions and discuss them in the same idiom ; where art connects instead of separating people ; where people feel, as in that new Salinger story, that every fat woman on earth is Jesus Christ; and where those who carry the torch of freedom are never asked to run with it into the ammunition dump? Do you want these things?'

When we came to London, it was a decade after *Look Back in Anger*. We looked around to see if the Establishment was still there. Was it distintegrating? Had it changed?

When we came to London, Harold Wilson had just won his second, impressive victory. After his first, close win, he had said to Mr. Anthony Sampson regarding 'the old Establishment':

'The Establishment can make noises, drinking gins and tonics at their New Year's Eve parties, but that doesn't have much effect on politics. Politics is a question of power, and power has been transferred. Whatever people say at an election, the members of the old Establishment only have one vote each at the end of the day. So has each engineer and miner in my constituency.'

Who, the world over, had not heard of the Angry Young Men? Who could and, as far as we were concerned, who would have wished to doubt Harold Wilson's words? We were dying to observe the upheavals which Britain was undergoing.

Our initial settling-in behind us, we plunged into British life and society. And what did we find? The dear old Establishment. Everywhere. Everyone.

It is getting weaker and weaker, we were told. It has been getting weaker for years, we were assured. Haven't you heard about universal suffrage? Don't you know that the great change began with the emergence of the parliamentary Labour Party? Don't you know that the old order began to break down as a result of World War I and large-scale conscription? Have you never read *Lady Chatterley's Lover*, a novel about Class no less than about Sex? The old aristocracy is impotent. The virile working-class is taking over.

Well, I don't know. When we took our first good look at it all, it was more than two decades after World War II and the Establishment—which was still dying—kept being around, kept capturing the imagination of the people, kept having its hold on much imaginary and most of the real power.

It may all be something of a circus, as Osborne puts it; but then isn't life but a stage, as an earlier playwright is known to have observed. Wilson had won on technology, on the promise of more schools, modernised industry, computers, balance of payments, but nothing sells a newspaper better than a colour supplement on the Queen or members of the aristocracy, and that, too, is a fact of life. Royalty may have little to do with ruling the country, yet one has the feeling that the only revolution ever likely to erupt in England will be against anyone with republican ideas. It is hard to conceive of a Communist British State with an ordinary Secretary-General and no Queen. I feel certain that the C.P. would have been far better off had they attached the word 'Royal' to their name—nothing would win them more love, prestige and trust than simply being known as 'The Royal Communist Party of Great Britain.'

Circus or no, the very use of the epithet Royal on a hotel or hospital, academy or pub adds enormously to its standing in the public eye—do not ask me why. Even in Israel, the most popular brand of cigarette—the very kind I am puffing at as I pen these words—is called just that: Royal. . . . And this attachment to royalty is not confined to things which bear the stamp of age, handed down from former, less sophisticated times. Many a new establishment or institution will consider itself extremely fortunate if entitled to associate its name in one way or another with the Court or if allowed to adorn its product with the magic label: 'By appointment to Her Majesty.'

As foreigners, we were somewhat surprised to note that nothing is worth noticing if it cannot be publicised as taking place under the patronage or in the presence of Her Majesty, His Royal Highness, one of the Royal Princesses, Dukes, or at least some titled nobleman. England has changed, they say, but tradition has not. Who would pretend that Ascot is no longer *the* event of summer, at which anybody who is somebody wishes to be seen, photographed, discussed? And then there are the Royal Shows at the

Palladium. To be presented to the Queen—on television—is the pinnacle of any Show Biz career. And then there is the ritual Opening of Parliament, with Royalty at the head of the procession. And then there are the summer Afternoon Parties given in the gardens of Buckingham Palace. And there is that most sparkling event—the Evening Reception for the Diplomatic Corps inside the Palace itself.

I must in all honesty admit that I, too, felt greatly excited on being introduced—first time ever—to a real flesh and blood life-peer. My knees shook when he actually addressed me; I was positively agitated to find myself seated next to him. Imagine my emotional state on entering the Palace—in full evening dress—through the Grand Entrance, through the gilded and chandeliered corridors of Royalty, in the company of all the Great, the men ablaze with ribbons, medals, decorations, the women twinkling, gem-adorned, in diamonded tiaras. Imagine us, Israeli commoners standing there in the Music Room, observing Her Majesty and other members of the Royal Family at such amazingly close quarters. When I wrote home to my father, describing that and similar events in my English life to him in great detail, he wrote back asking me whether I had pronounced the blessing incumbent upon a pious Jew on viewing royal personages. No, Royalty is no laughing matter, say what you will; and please do not tell me that all those dukes and earls are mere flesh and blood. I have seen writers and poets of note—whose identity shall not be revealed here—who, upon uttering the word 'Princess' (and they were not referring to the Austin car), would break into verse. Yes, my friends, even in this cool, sophisticated, vulgar, materialistic twentieth century of ours, a lord is a lord is a lord. And anyone who knows his Dickens knows that an English lord cannot be compared with any other nobleman—not Tolstoy's graff, de Balzac's marquis, the German baron. For a lord is something quite unique.

What is a lord?

We could see that it was not only the Court alone which was permanently in the limelight, for the public and the popular press to thrive on. Their insatiable passion for every detail about the Great, their hankering for glamour, goes beyond the Royal Family. In other countries, this need is focused largely on celebrities of the cinema and sports ; in England there is the aristocracy, old and new, titled or otherwise. It is this kind of hierarchy that one has in mind when the issue of an Establishment comes up. Now I know that to say of someone that he is a lord is to say almost nothing, except that he is not a commoner, which seems to mean something even to a die-hard leftist Life Peer. And I know that of the many lords who people Shakespeare's dramas barely a handful have survived. Why, even the dukes are lacking in a pedigree which reaches back to the bygone days before Henry VIII established his new order, temporal and secular. There are less than two hundred lords who can trace their aristocratic origin to the eighteenth century and more than half are twentieth-century innovations. This has been the British way of keeping things in place: by injecting red-blooded capitalist resources into the blue veins of the nobility. This is the Establishment.

Or is it ? Is there a clear, cut and dried distinction between the Old Establishment and the New ? There must be, yet there also seems to be something there which tends to make even the new look old, the most radical idea sound as entrenched and established within the English Way of Life as the Tower of London.

Occasionally one will hear voices of protest against the privileged hereditary aristocracy, or the House of Lords might come under fire from the Left. Yet nothing is really going to be done about it all, except in the English way of pouring new wine into the old vessel. On the one hand, the Lords has very little power left. On the other, is there a nicer way of kicking upwards an old party leader, a trade union man, a distinguished socialist barrister, a helpful financier ?

It is a matter of some moment, for Mr. So-and-so, known to his friends as George, to be elevated to the Peerage. He is reborn—with a new name, new stationery, signing only his last, very last, name. He may continue to be the same old George, but henceforth his presence will be much in demand at all kinds of dinners in honour of this and that ; he will be much importuned by a variety of good-doing bodies of one kind or another; and his appearance as guest of honour on some such occasion will be signalled by the Master of Ceremonies (red livery, the moustache and voice of a Sergeant-Major) calling out: 'Pray silence for the Righ Honourable the Lord So-and-so of Swiss Cottage.' It is no simple matter. Not at all simple.

We had often visualised the Establishment—in the shape of an ancient castle, a dark maze of halls and cloisters, covered with cobwebs and dusty coats-of-arms, haunted by ghosts, resounding with voices from a long dead past. And then we chanced to stray into the labyrinthine corridors of power and, lo and behold! What is it that we encounter? Skyscrapers in steel-glass-chromium; giant computers and the other instruments of science and technology; cool and calculatingly efficient executives, their time weighed in gold; supremely professional men of business managing vast financial empires mightier than the mightiest feudal duchy.

All one has to do is open one's eyes and see the City. I had vivid memories of our first visit to London fifteen years earlier, when the ruins and the rubble and the huge empty lots were to be seen everywhere. This is where the new London has emerged, American style, an assault upon the eyes of the lovers of old England, with its banks, insurance companies, its huge Shell complex on the south bank. It's the same all over the country. The English are as circumspect as ever, try to pretend that all is as it used to be. But is anything the same as it used to be? One sees the same eruption in Manchester and Liverpool, in Leeds and Glasgow, in all the many New Towns, in the sprawling suburbia, the motorways, the airports. Even Cambridge and Oxford, those citadels of England the eternal, are not quite what they used to be; you see it in their architecture, you notice it in the contents and purpose of their curriculum. The old ideal of educating a gentleman and dilettante who would be good at anything from the colonial and foreign service to politics, from art to business to soldiering—such an ideal runs counter to what the new England needs or wants, to what the new Establishment feels is necessary for itself, and for the country.

And it is at this point that the government and the

new Establishment seem to meet, somehow: in the giant corporations, the technocrats, banks, contractors, insurance companies, the individualistic enterprises of the post-war tycoons. Do they, between them, constitute the *real* Establishment? How can an outsider tell? All he can do is observe appearances. And it would appear that the new Establishment and the government—whether Conservative or Socialist—do not really wish to tear down the old fabric of society. They would like to take it over as it stands, to be admitted into the innermost chambers of the old establishment so completely that henceforth they would be it.

Who are *they?* Anonymous corporations with a turn-over of millions, employing hundreds of thousands in their giant enterprises, countries in themselves. Consider Shell, Unilever, I.C.I., Great Universal Stores, Marks & Spencer's, Burton's, Sainsbury's and the hundreds of others of their like, some no older than this century, others that came of age after World War II. Consider the great banking establishments, founded by pious and prudent Quaker folk. Between them, they command a power which makes them into an Establishment all of its own. Consider the great merchant bankers: the Rothschilds come to mind immediately, but the group has several recently-acquired members, too, such as Hill, Samuel or Sir Siegmund Warburg, who began operating in the City only after World War II. Consider the huge building enterprises, contractors, real estate tycoons—heirs to neither wealth nor name but true sons of their times: shrewd, sharp and agile, buying today what the market will demand tomorrow, selling tomorrow options bought yesterday, wedding property to capital, changing the face of cities, building themselves up high as their skyscrapers. Consider the people of show business, men who began their million-pound march with a few shillings in their pocket—as actors, store-keepers, theatre owners—who today are the lords of the West End, of Granada, Thames and Associated Television.

Are all these no more than faceless corporations? After one has been in London for a while, the names of the people behind these giant citadels of power begin to lose their anonymity. One sees and hears more and more of them, as great patrons of the arts and universities, as people whose ambition no longer lies in the mere amassing of more money but in converting wealth into political power, in gaining control of the strongholds of the Establishment.

I see the faces. I remember the dinners. I recall the names of donors to art galleries, new college buildings, to any and every good cause imaginable. They are for the most part the newcomers. Their names appear in the annual list of peerages, knighthoods, C.B.E.s, they are granted the freedom of cities, are the recipients of honorary Ph.D.s, they are desperately intent on ageing, anxious to become proper old Establishment.

Are they *it*?

Well, since the old is itself not very old, and the new needs only time in order to grow old, the problem is not all that complicated. Status is always hard-pressed for cash, and money will pay handsomely for pedigree. It is in keeping with the English tradition for the two camps to co-exist in a sort of symbiosis. The aristocratic principle seems to be accepted not only by the aristocrats themselves but—and perhaps more importantly—by the working classes. It is still quite generally believed that they, the upper classes, know best how to run the country, that they are uniquely fitted for government by background, upbringing, education, values. A short sketch I once saw on the David Frost show seemed to me to sum it all up quite pithily: there were three characters standing in line—one very tall, the second very short, the third of medium height. Said the tall one: 'I look down on the middle class.' Said the medium one: 'I look up to the upper class.' Said the short one: 'I know my place.'

The real source of friction within the Establishment is between the upper and the middle class. The newcomers not only accept the aristocratic outlook, they attempt to adopt it and endeavour to turn their children into 'worthies' —give them the right kind of education, upbringing and environment, groom them into the natural confidence which they themselves so sorely envy.

We visited numerous schools and universities, talked to people concerned with education, tried to understand the

Labour Party's policy regarding comprehensive schooling and the establishment of new universities. There can be little doubt—and statistical evidence supports the claim—that the select public and grammar schools, on the one hand, and Oxford and Cambridge on the other, are as much as ever the nursing grounds of the Establishment. The truly select public schools admit but a fraction of one per cent of any given year-group. One need only look at the social and scholastic background of either the present government or its Socialist predecessor to realise that the Establishment may, after all, be more than just a word.

Did we ever find it?

I wish I knew. At times I thought it was somewhere else. Driving across the country, I would think that it resided in the fact that every bed-and-breakfast table was an exact replica of the next: same food, same cutlery, same bottle of ketchup and mustard. At times I would think it lay in the pubs, from Dover to Liverpool, from the docks to Hampstead Heath. Despite all the differences, despite the many changes, England looked to me an eminently established, past-dominated country. It may be very different from what it was a century or even a mere three decades ago, yet to an Israeli who thinks in terms of either thousands of years back or of no more than sixty years or so, England seemed to be the one and only country in which the word 'new' sounds natural in association with a college founded four hundred years ago. When all new things were established, including the Establishment.

After all, we are talking about a country where one accepts as sufficient reason for not doing something the statement: 'It isn't done.'

Or is it?

LONDON BRIDGE IS COMING DOWN

London Bridge is coming down,
Coming down,
Coming down,
It's off to Arizona . . .

NOTHING SEEMED more indicative of the bitter-dry mood of Britain's younger generation than the words-cum-music of this pop-song's gay off-beat proclaiming of the passing of yet another of the symbols of Imperial London. The bridge had been sold to Americans, to be pulled down and shipped off, stone by stone, to the desert state of Arizona, there to be put up again—over some dry canyon, no doubt—and resurrected as a major tourist attraction of the American south-west.

That the said London Bridge is not the one alluded to in the old tales is of little comfort. Nor is the fact that it is not the one celebrated on a multitude of picture post-cards —which is Tower Bridge. Nor are Englishmen heartened by the sound business side of the deal : the bridge was due to be pulled down, anyway, to make room for a new-fangled construction more fitting to the age. Besides, those simpletons from the Wild West not only removed its unwanted stones from sight, they even paid a million and a half pounds for the privilege. . . .

Such considerations are immaterial. What seems to impress people is the symbolism of the thing. When the brash young pop-singers warble the words 'coming down, coming down,' it is a stab in the heart of every Englishman. One cannot help but see it as yet another sign of the passing of the Britannia that once ruled the waves—giving place to a little England knocking on the doors of the Common Market, surrendering her last outposts east of Suez, painfully witnessing the growing prosperity of her vanquished foes of yesteryear, Germany and Japan, desperately continuing to act at playing the great roles which gave her an everlasting name in the world theatre—in a world that has gone for ever. The stage has changed, and one by one each of the appurtenances of power vanishes, at times to the tune of a last bugle-call, for the most part unnoticed.

It is no secret that the Royal Navy is no longer mistress of the seven seas, that the Merchant Navy is no longer the greatest of them all. We all know the story of how Peter the Great of Russia went to England to study ship-building, inspired by the conviction that the setting up of a sizeable fleet was a crucial step in the transformation of his land-locked realm into a major power; today the Russians are doing their best to make the Czarist dream come true—their fleet by now is second only to one. Yet when the *Queen Mary* embarked on her last voyage—relegated to the role of floating hotel, entertainment and convention centre off the Los Angeles beach—there was a certain poignancy about it, as if they'd sold the Crown Jewels, almost. The records set by the once-great liner—for speed, for sumptuousness, for the illustriousness of her passenger-list—had, in the 'thirties, been symbolic of Britain's supremacy at sea and abroad. Today the 'Queen' is simply not a paying proposition—she is old-fashioned and out of gear with the times, and what remains of her former elegance just does not appeal to the taste and pace of the jet-set 'seventies. Old glory—with the stress on old. We too, like many an Englishman, accompanied her via the television screen on her last voyage en route to a Grade-B type living in Los Angeles. *Sic transit gloria mundi.*

We mentioned the Colonial Office in an earlier chapter. To us, living in the Jewish National Home, it seemed the centre of the universe, the seat of power where all major decisions were unalterably taken. The same bloated mass of a Victorian edifice is still there today, across a square inner courtyard from the Foreign Office, its blackish stone walls adorned with the graven images of mighty Empire builders —from the colonisation of America to the but recent scramble for Africa and the Middle East; its impressive corridors and halls are still lined with huge oils depicting centuries of bold adventurers, brave, shrewd and venal sailors, soldiers, clerks, missionaries. But the Colonial Office as such is a redundancy. Even the Ministry meant to replace it—for Commonwealth Affairs—aged almost in a night and was forthwith incorporated into the Foreign Office.

These are but three of the many symbols of yesteryear, all fallen before the incredulous eyes of a single generation. It was only yesterday that the subjects and liegemen of the British Crown gathered together from every corner of the earth entire for the coronation of George the Sixth, King by the Grace of God, Defender of the Faith, Emperor of India. That splendid hour looks to us today like a blind man's masque held in a house on fire, not unlike the ironic opening scene of *King Lear*. When George VI passed away a mere fifteen years later, he left behind a different Britain, wounded, maimed, a country in which nothing was what it had been on his Coronation Day in Westminster Abbey. Yet not only the old were affected. Even those of us who were children in the 'thirties can remember how, at school, the red of the Empire dominated the world-map. And what about all the thousands in the Colonial Service—the regular army officers and those who peopled the various administrations and police forces—who returned to a Britain swamped with millions of demobilised ex-servicemen, a Britain in the throes of post-war reconstruction, of rations and housing shortage and all that sense of shock and loss to contend with?

It was against this background that the angry young men emerged—no more than an initial indication of what the post-war generation was undergoing. We gradually came to appreciate the force of the tremors which seemed to be imperilling the very foundations of that Establishment whose flexibility, adaptability and durability had both amazed and awed us so.

And again, what is the Establishment? Not only the Court, not only the aristocracy old and new, not only the education system of-by-and-for the élite. The Establishment is also last year's rebels—Left-wing politicians and non-conforming writers included. In an earlier chapter, I mentioned the 'Declaration' of Osborne, Tynan, *et al.* Their younger siblings regard them as bastions of the Establishment, though they themselves may still feebly protest against such calumny. Perhaps they have been embraced by the Establishment. After all, that is the English way of doing things. If you can't beat the Beatles, include them in the Honours List. Kenneth Tynan started to set the tone at the National Theatre, and the national press and other media were quick to cash in on the new mood. In an interview with Kenneth Harris for *The Observer,* John Osborne said something—and I do not quote—to the effect that he was lucky to escape the working-class. The two latest plays of his which I managed to see, *Time Present* and *Hotel in Amsterdam,* were a far cry from the play which gave a name to a generation. Particularly illuminating was his contribution to an *Encounter* discussion on 'Intellectuals and Just Causes,' published in the wake of the Six-Day War (September, 1967). For me, both as a curious foreigner and as a much-involved Israeli, the following lines were interesting:

'The last time I involved myself in any political demonstration was in 1961 when, with a great many other writers or hang-around writers, I "sat down" in Trafalgar Square.... I resolved then that I should never engage in this kind of concerted affair again unless some unforeseeable situation should arise.... I have long refused to sign those glib and predictable letters to *The Times,* including the one during the recent Israeli crisis when so many of these cause-happy activists leapt to the telephone and to their pens.

'The same principle applies to the Vietnam War, the very name of which has become a synonym for Left-wing sanctimony. I have not been able to come to a clear resolution over these or many other political dilemmas. I do know I have little to choose between Communist police terrorism and shoddy American power politics. Except that I find the latter minimally less repugnant.... Consequently I sign letters no longer, friends who were never friends call me blimp. To hell with them....'

One may agree or disagree with Osborne. He ends his

contribution by announcing that he is not going to give money to 'subsidise ungifted people who organise these junkets.' After consideration, he concludes that he would do better to spend his earnings on a subscription ' to *Horse and Hound* and a girl to read it with.' One may agree or disagree, but one has no difficulty in placing him *vis-à-vis* the angry young men of the late 'sixties whom we met in London.

Another contributor to the 'Declaration,' Kenneth Tynan, has written about his return to Oxford to do a programme for television; his encounter with the present-day rebels—as described in an article in *The Observer*—was no less revealing. He had been a member of the post-war group at Oxford, a distinction shared with some of the best-known names of today's Establishment, Left and Right alike, several of whom he mentions there—Anthony Wedgwood Benn, Sir Edward Boyle, Paul Johnson, Tony Richardson, John Schlesinger, Kingsley Amis and others. Back at Oxford, Tynan asked the latter-day rebels what they thought of his generation of angry young. The leader of student-revolt does not hesitate : to him, Tynan and his like are nothing but servants of the established régime. The young Right-wingers dismiss them as mere light-weights—the kind who never give the régime real cause for concern. Tynan—who seems to have forgotten his letter to a young student published in ' Declaration '—admits that his generation was not ' militant' in the sense that the term is understood by the rebel-leader and his followers. Oxford moulded them, and in the process taught them where the permissible limits of controversy lie. The angry young men of today want to turn Oxford upside down, seeing therein the first step towards the rearrangement of society as a whole.

One wonders whether these young people actually have any social plan or programme, whether they have any clear and positively orientated idea as to the society they want, and the ways they intend to accomplish it. There is, however, one immediate impression which tends to surprise the foreigner who has been to England on an earlier occasion, or who thought he knew all about it : an entire generation has put the veto on the traditional, the socially accepted, that which is or used to be taken-for-granted. They seem to be saying: I may not know precisely who I am, but get this clear—if that's how *you* are, then I'm different.

Oh, yes, the City is still there, and the Inns of Court are still there, and the Clubs, and the never-changing menu, and the concrete-reinforced class barriers, and tradition and ceremony and strict formalities. But at a two-minutes' walk from the Athenaeum there is Carnaby Street, where you are either a mini or a maxi, where you can buy every imaginable kind of garment except for a good solid English wool suit, where they sell you the Union Jack—painted on kitchen-mitts and dustbins.

Rebellion and dissent are symbolised by the Beatles, the Rolling Stones, the flower people, the drop-outs—but mostly by the Beatles, who seem to have given legitimate expression to the illegitimate, to being different, and to have done so far more effectively than the theatre and the other arts. They constituted the Royal Court of the post-war slum-children of Liverpool, of the children born to the tired heroes of the army and the navy and the RAF, of those born in servantless country-homes and town-houses. The provocative, nervous, jangling beat of the Beatles stamped out the saccharine sentimentality of tunes beloved by their fathers and grandfathers, their unkempt hair and anti-conventional dress were the complete antithesis of the nice English schoolboy in his dull, inevitable school uniform, with his neatly shorn hair so carefully slicked down and parted, the kind of young person who should be seen, never heard. They are the craving for something which may be indefinable, possibly unattainable, but which most certainly is *not a* nice secure job in the Church or Army, in the Civil Service, the City or in Politics. They quite evidently reject that once omnipotent maxim 'What was good enough for my father is good enough for me.' Only being different is good enough.

I recall an evening in Stratford-upon-Avon, where we spent a long autumn week-end, staying in a small family hotel, devouring one Shakespearian play after the other, relishing the flavour of the picturesque. We did not mind the fact that the town was heavily tourist-orientated, or that much of its Tudor architecture was no more than a latter-day face-lift. The deep silence in the small dining-hall, broken only by the clinking of silver on the wedgwood ware, the swans on the Avon, the hum of the audience during the interval out on the open balcony of the theatre, the memory of a manor-house we had visited in the afternoon—all combined into a feeling of timeless England, of the Great Will, of David Garrick, whose deserted villa in Hampton Court we used to pass on our way to friends who lived near by on the Thames.

And then we came out into the drizzle, and were on the road leading along the Avon from the theatre back to our hotel. A gang of young hoodlums on their motor-cycles, sporting their leather-coats and crash-helmets, sounding their exhausts and horns raucously, were challenging—or already fighting—another group of youngsters. People seemed anxious to avoid them, not to get involved, to have no part of this naked brutality obviously looking for an outlet. They seemed several light-years away from what to us had appeared so predominantly English.

I recall how my son, who was thirteen at the time and already greatly impressed by the Beatle sub-culture, explained to me the difference between the Teddy-boys and Rock-'n'-Roll on the one hand and the essentially non-violent attitude of the Beatles and the flower people, on the other. They may be uninhibited, they may reject totally and ecstatically the norms of the established order, but what they really ache for is something different, liberated, honest, something which they so often epitomise in that ancient over-exploited word 'love.' I am not quoting what my son said, but that was what he wanted to say. Where, I could not help asking myself that evening in Stratford-upon-Avon, and in Chelsea, and in Notting Hill Gate, and when considering the timid student outburst which followed the May Revolution in Paris, where was the heart of England's angry young man?

Close observation of the behaviour of groups labelled 'the fringe' is helpful in trying to understand a host of other phenomena, not so extreme and not so powerful in impact. One has the clear impression that there is a general re-appraisal of values, a re-evaluation which leaves not a stone unturned. The fundamental change in Britain's role in the world today forms the main undercurrent of the new plays, at the theatre, on television. The English play prior to the World War II was essentially for and about the middle-class, given that the upper-class did not very much care for it and the lower-class could not afford it. This is as true of Shaw as of Maugham and Noel Coward. The emergence of television as a literally mass medium must have performed a very special role in England. Take *Pygmalion*, for instance, where language figures as both a class symbol and a dramatic force. It would be seen by theatre-goers who were largely educated middle-class, and who had a full appreciation of Eliza Doolittle's struggle to be 'accepted.' They would also enjoy the comic effect of cockney, used by Shaw in the time-honoured tradition of bringing the lower-class on stage for purposes of comedy, never 'drama.' The market people of Covent Garden were not theatre-goers—and had they gone, they would have failed to get the joke.

Television is there for everyone, for both Eliza and her dad; and they and their kind form the bulk of England's set-owners. A Liverpool labourer does not find his own accent funny, nor does a London docker or a Welsh miner. He may find the language as well as the problems of a middle-class woman suffering from boredom rather more amusing. And his life, as far as he is concerned, *has* drama, has its tragedies. Talking posh may arouse respect, but it also raises a barrier, makes a person feel uneasy, estranges the set from its owner. Having such a distinguished guest settled permanently in one's living-room may be something of an embarrassment. After all, a man does not dress up in his Sunday best before he turns it on. It is there when one is one's own self, in open-necked shirt and slippers, having a beer or a cup of tea, maybe even a family row. It joins the family, and one wants it to behave like a member of the family, acting natural.

Friends of mine connected with the television world pointed out some of these features of the medium to me. They tell me, too, that one of the results of television's campaign for the soul of every viewer has been to blunt the sharp edges of the 'Pygmalion complex' in British society.

It has given rise to a whole host of series and of serials peopled by common-folk whose problems are Coronation Street, whose language is Alf Garnett, whose heroes are Tom, Dick and Harry.

A foreigner can train his ear so that after a year or so he himself becomes a quasi-Professor Higgins, able to pin-point a person's class, education, background simply by hearing him talk. Englishmen carry their identity on the tip of their tongue. The newer playwrights—Osborne, Wesker, Kopps, Pinter, Mercer, as well as others who write almost exclusively for television—have contributed to a certain inversion of the Pygmalion complex, so much so that it is not uncommon to see politicians and other public figures of impeccable upper-class origins now trying very hard to lose their 'posh' style of speech, to sound as folksy as is humanly possible for them.

Liberation from conventions of the past is noticeable in the defiant rejection of all and anything smacking of Victorian prudery. One need merely note the zeal invested in recent legislation concerning 'consenting adults' and the complete abolition of censorship on plays. Some say Britain has become the most permissive country in the world; one might perhaps put it rather differently—permissiveness is no longer restricted to the upper-class.

Such heart-searching seems to have touched on every area of life. The assault on public schools and on the select grammar school is a case in point. Going comprehensive was conceived as the best and only way of narrowing class gaps perpetuated by the traditional structure of British education, which had given much to the few and very little to the many. The same equalising aim lay behind the rapid expansion of the universities, and the development of large-scale housing projects, health and welfare services. The emphasis on the under-privileged, as against the traditional orientation towards the over-privileged, was manifest in the widened scope of the Arts Council as well as in the appointment by the Labour Government, of Jennie Lee as Minister in charge of the Arts (the Government viewing its role as not 'to dictate taste or restrict the liberty of even the most unorthodox and experimental of artists,' but as to support the arts so that a high level of artistic achievement can be sustained and the best in the arts made more widely available).

These fresh approaches reflected more than a progressive outlook on the part of a Labour Government back in power after many years in the cold; they signified additionally—perhaps primarily—its recognition of the surprising explosion of creativity in contemporary England, a country supposedly in the throes of a profound psychological upheaval. That there has been a most striking renaissance in the arts needs no elaboration. It is not only that the theatre has been rejuvenated. Henry Moore and Barbara Hepworth have introduced new dimensions into modern art. Ted Hughes and Philip Larkin are only two of an exciting new generation of poets. But it is more than that. London seems to have taken over the place traditionally held by Paris as Mecca of the young, the venturesome, the *avant-garde*. The revolution of the young has left its mark in London—perhaps more than in any other capital—on fashion, on shop-windows, even on popular cafeterias like the Wimpey Houses, which are so different from their forerunners — Lyons and the A.B.C. Compared with King's Road, the Left Bank of Paris is backward and pedestrian. Poetry readings and jazz concerts are not confined to bohemian hang-outs or the universities; they attract the young people of suburbia into the new community centres, too. Britain has evidently at long last made the break with tradition in the field of architecture: one sees this on the South Bank, in Coventry Cathedral, on various university campuses. The fringe, the *avant-garde,* the anti-establishmentarian have become the source of a new and unexpected type of glory for Little England.

And so the Establishment, which ought to have vanished along with the world of yesteryear, once again proved how incredible a thing was English adaptability. In medieval times, rival dynasties and upstart pretenders were constantly fighting things out with one another, and life was pretty violent. Yet it was Britain that first put a stop—long before the French, let alone the Russians—to the beheading of kings. After Cromwell failed to establish a Republic, and after the Stuarts failed to re-establish themselves on the throne, all those concerned came to prefer less risky methods of retaining power. No use drowning a revolution in blood, better handle it with care and patience, drown it in an ocean of affection. Innovations are not necessarily a danger in themselves, as long as they can be moulded into the patterns of tradition. If you wish to avoid taking measures against violators of the law—all you have to do is amend the law. And if all other attempts to restrain insurgents against the Crown fail—knight them. The system worked wonderfully well in the past, and it seems to still be working wonders nowadays.

I recall particularly one occasion—the reception held at the Tate Gallery after Norman Reed had taken over and re-arranged it radically to reflect contemporary trends in art. Works which had for years been on show in the main halls of the gallery were now relegated to places of less prominence —or else stacked away in the cellars or simply handed over to other institutions—and the central show places were thrown wide open to representatives of every variety of modernistic experimentation: op, pop, kinetic art, assemblages, collages and all the rest. This revolutionary re-arrangement was celebrated on that memorable evening in the presence of Her Majesty, with the cream of London's upper social and artistic crust turned out in black tie and dazzling evening-dress, with candle-lights and silver and ice-chilled champagne. One would have thought it to be a most awkward kind of juxtapositioning—Royalty and gracious bows and curtseyings alongside weirdly revolving contraptions, dancing lines and shapes, comic-strip figures and fantasies. One would have thought Side A would view rubbing elbows with Side B with the utmost distaste, and vice versa. Yet that was not the case at all on that superbly elegant, glittering, intoxicating evening of cultural éclat. Everyone came out a winner: the Establishment dragged the *avant-garde* away from the fringe and set it squarely in the heart of society, while the latter for their part furnished the Establishment with an up-dated, modern, cultured image fitting to the spirit of the changing times.

London Bridge is coming down . . . and new bridges are spanned above it. There is a revolt against the old—and a hankering after it. There is disdain for anything sanctioned by the Establishment—and a burning desire to enjoy all it has to offer, both real and illusory. The Beatles drive the same Rolls-Royces, even if they have had them painted psychedelic. The student rebels wear their fair hair long, and one has a suspicion that they might be wishing to emulate an earlier breed of true Anglo-Saxons, the gallant Knights of the Round Table, the chivalrous Crusaders, or other heroes of England's finest hours. They have nothing but contempt for a Burton suit, so they do their day-dreaming in the tunics of the Light Brigade. When all is said and done, there is something utterly romantic about this lost generation. Their hearts ache for Old Glory. Very much so.

I am reminded of a television series, the plot of which I managed to watch before I left for home, and of what the man in charge of scripts told me at the time. Lately, said my writer-friend, one notices a certain reaction against all this passion for destroying whatever was cherished and sacred to earlier generations. So we have decided to try out something rather different, something that on the face of it might seem to run completely counter to the spirit of our time. We're going to do a series about the Indian Frontier during the hey-day of the British Raj. Yes, plain and simply out of respect for those brave and gallant Britishers. . . . Yes, out of honest, unabashed nostalgia. . . .

The plot, which my friend hoped would unfold week by week, from one adventure to the next, from war to love and back again, to the delight of (hopefully) millions of Britons looking back not in anger, but in sorrow and longing for what had gone with the Eastern wind, went as follows: a young officer, born into a family whose self-respecting sons had all served in India, embarks on a voyage which is to add further glory to his noble family, warmed by the blessings and affections of his Victorian aunts. It was obvious from the outset that this series would differ in some respects from the Indian adventure films of the 'thirties based on Kipling's novels and the like. The officers figuring in this show included a 'political officer,' and one of the goodies is himself an Anglo-Indian—from which it follows that he is by no means a colonialist but an Indian patriot serving the best interests of his Asian motherland. . . .

This minor feature of the film is no mere accident; for while television viewers include ex-colonial civil servants, policemen and missionaries, these days they also include hundreds of thousands of immigrants from the Indian subcontinent, from the West Indies, Africa and other parts of what used to be the Empire. All this has to be taken into account when one tries to captivate an audience; one needs to consider the immigrants as well as those native Englishmen who are completely anti-coloured immigration, nor can one ignore the distressing tensions which have arisen between the English and other groups that have recently started making their own national identity felt in the country. We shall come back to this latter point. All I would wish to say in passing is that this, too, is a sign of the times, a symptom of the conflict between old and new, between the permanent and long-established and the mood of change, a mood which may be more than fleeting.

London Bridge is coming down. . . .

THE CELTIC LEAGUE AND
ELIEZER BEN YEHUDA

AN ODD ASSORTMENT of invitations used to reach my desk. One day I came upon a most official-looking document with an elegant green letter-head in English and some other language which turned out to be—yes, one of the Gaelic tongues. The letter itself was a cordial invitation to give a talk on the revival of Hebrew to the members of the Celtic League. They had long been fascinated by the phenomenon of Modern Hebrew, ran the letter, and would I be so kind as to come and enlighten them as to how we had contrived it.

I, of course, accepted the invitation gladly and forthwith, in good British form, despatched a formal letter thanking them for their kind consideration. I no less promptly received a letter in good Celtic form graciously acknowledging receipt of my reply and would such-and-such a date be convenient. I thereupon sent off another letter saying that the date suited me perfectly, and received a reply in confirmation of my confirmation. As the scheduled date approached, I obtained a reminder in writing and several by telephone, to all of which I replied both promptly and politely. I had clearly become involved with a highly business-like and very earnest league.

I shall spare the reader the details of my frantic quest for the League headquarters, down a never-ending street with houses numbered, not by the natural sequence of from one on and up to infinity, but according to some quite unfathomable code. Fortunately, I did manage to find the house at last, though by then a little late. It was one of those Georgian houses, where you go up a short flight of steps above pavement level, or else down a long flight of steps into the servants' quarters. There was a long panel of door-bells out in front, but no sign of the League. I was just about ready to give the whole thing up when a man appeared on the stairs leading from the basement and enquired anxiously whether I were the distinguished guest. I was. 'And I,' my companion introduced himself in the half-darkness. 'I have been asked to chair the meeting for our secretary. He himself is unable to attend owing to a bad cold. Most unfortunate,' added the poor chap, who himself sounded in rather less than the best of health. I assured him that I quite understood and followed him down into the basement.

We entered a damp, ill-lit passage and walked past a drab little room through whose open door I caught a glimpse of pamphlets, stacks of papers, scattered chairs and sundry other familiar accessories of a revolutionary cell. We went into the next room, a slightly larger version of the first. This one had an old piano squashed in near one wall, a small table covered with a green map—presumably for my benefit —and two rows of chairs. My acting-secretary companion introduced the audience—each and every one a Celt, from Scotland, Wales, Cornwall, Ireland, the Isle of Man. They had a Breton, too, but he had been unable to attend for one reason or another. They numbered eight in all, including the chairman of the evening—representatives of the various subjugated minorities of the United Kingdom.

I found the circumstances rather disconcerting, in view of the lengthy and punctilious correspondence on official paper with green, bilingual letter-heads which had preceded. Having got this far, I decided to take the line of least resistance and get the thing over with as amiably and effectively as possible. The proceedings opened with a few words of apology from the chairman, who begged me not to be misled by the scant attendance. The latter could be attributed to any number of factors, none of which had the least bearing upon either the weightiness of the evening's topic or the intensity of nationalist feeling in the regions represented by the members of my audience. The chairman then proceeded to deliver a brief discourse of his own concerning the revival of the Hebrew language—a subject with which, to my surprise, he proved to be thoroughly conversant. Then I got up and gave the talk I had prepared, the unforeseen circumstances notwithstanding. That done, question-time began. The questions were mainly of a practical purpose: How had we been so successful? What had we done? How were textbooks compiled? Who trained the teachers? Does Hebrew meet the needs of modern man? There were only eight of them, but eight hundred could not have posed more questions, encompassed a wider range of topics, stuck harder to the same central theme—the revival of the dead Gaelic tongues.

They were an odd collection—a handful of intent, solemn-faced men assembled in a drab, damp basement. One felt inclined to dismiss them all with a sceptical shrug. Yet there was something about them that was reminiscent of our own zealous Hebraists of the early nineteen-hundreds. Specially so the chairman, who knew all about the life-story of the Ben Yehuda family and their linguistic exploits— incited by a stern and stubborn father to speak, read, write and think in pure, unmitigated Hebrew in an environment of Arabic and Yiddish. My chairman struggled bravely to establish an analogy, yet I could not help feeling—perhaps with unwarranted Israeli arrogance—that they did not really have all that much confidence in their chances of success. For my part, I carefully did and said nothing that might undermine the United Kingdom or promote separatist insurrection. As a foreign diplomat, I kept strictly to factual information and to waiting for the evening to end.

And, sure enough, it did come to an end. One of the two Irishmen stood up and announced that he was going to play *Hatikva* in my honour. Whereupon he sat down at the piano and played our anthem through from start to finish. The remaining seven rose to attention, while the pianist and the chairman sang the words, in Hebrew. At first I felt rather silly, but then I joined in too. It was all a bit absurd, yet as a Hebrew-speaking, thinking, writing Israeli, I experienced a certain sense of euphoria, even of great pride. The naïve, time-worn words of *Hatikva* rang out as though some magic incantation. I did not say what I was thinking, that there was an important difference between our situation and theirs.

I did not say that I was afraid the incantation would not work. Why say such things?

I recalled another visit made some time before to a Welsh club—in Gray's Inn Road, if I'm not mistaken. A huge, bare hall. Half a dozen youngsters aged from six to fourteen or so were busy rehearsing something in Welsh, under the tutelage of an enthusiastic young woman. You could tell that their parents had made them come. You could see that they were bored stiff. 'Why Welsh, for heaven's sake?' I wondered. But I caught myself just in time. Who am *I*, of all people, to ask a thing like that!

I left the meeting-place with scarcely another thought for those eight gallant knights of the Gaelic tongue. But they remembered me. Not only they. A few weeks later, a letter came for me from Ireland, from the government department in charge of the revival of Irish, with a request for instructional material on the teaching of Hebrew. The writer referred to my talk, and mentioned the name of one of the eight. It may have been the pianist, who knows. A stubborn race, a stiff-necked people.

HER MAJESTY'S SOCIALIST GOVERNMENT

TO WRITE about Socialist Governments in Britain has always been a hazardous undertaking. When the Hebrew edition of this book went to press, the Wilson Government was not only very much alive, but most posters and trend-watchers were of the view that the drastic measures taken by the Labour Government were beginning to pay off. The victory of 1966 might not repeat itself, but the worst, as indicated by successive by-elections, was over and there was a definite turn of the tide. Moreover, it so happened that days before the 1970 election I was back in London for a week or so, and when there quizzed all my friends, among them those who wished Labour out of Parliament altogether. They were all convinced of Labour's victory and accordingly placed their bets at Ladbroke's—who must have known better.

This preamble is an attempt to explain the problem I had on my hands when preparing the English version of this book. By the time I reached this page, Socialist Government in England was again a matter for historians and futurists. But since I have come neither to praise it in Hebrew nor to bury it in English, I feel that I may do now what I did then—keep wondering.

We landed in London—let it be repeated—only days after Harold Wilson's second, impressive victory, and in this we considered ourselves extremely fortunate. To be able to observe the working of a Socialist Monarchy in which the Upper Classes are still very Up and in which everybody else still knows his place was something to look forward to. After all, although the Parliamentary Labour Party was almost as old as our century, it had known only brief periods of power, and except for the Attlee Government it would prefer to forget them. Now that it had been given the Tools, it would get down, at long last, to doing the Job. Recalling the pre-1964 election speeches on the transformation of Britain into a modern, technology-science-and-education-minded society, one held one's breath with the suspense of watching Harold the Transformer, not just the reformer. One thought of the brush-off Wilson had given, in an interview, to the Old Establishment. Who, but Labour, was the agent of the winds of change, if change was really what England wanted? Was not Wilson the right man in the right time?

Proceeding cautiously through the corridors of the Establishment, across tradition-laden chambers, past bewigged guardians of time-honoured laws and customs, one opened many doors, creaking on their ancient hinges, looking for the New Society. Was it King's Road fashion? Was it the bio-chemical laboratory, in which a young brain was engaged in feverish pre-Nobel Prize activity? Or was it the reconstructed Manor House passed over from its original Tudor owner to a West End producer thrust from penury into wealth by a single musical? The Establishment old as well as new, was very visible. But how would one recognise Socialism when one saw it ? Which of the figures one encountered were fugitives from Madame Tussaud's, and which were the protagonists of contemporary drama?

I come from a polarly different society, in which history is ancient and sociology is partly present, partly future. Israel is not a Socialist State, and it has more strata than it had twenty years ago, but class has very limited meaning there. Moreover, the country may not be egalitarian, but the idea of a just society is a basic component of the country's ethos, by no means limited to the kibbutz or to the many diversified social, economic and trade union organisations. I suspect that even right-wing parties, committed to free enterprise and all that goes with it, hardly represent class in the sense Englishmen understand it. To have in your passport as occupation 'agricultural labourer', even though you may have been for many years a distinguished public figure, is still pedigree. To have in your biography—be you a wealthy businessman or a right-wing politician—a few years of manual labour, of humble existence, of membership of a kibbutz, is tantamount to tracing one's ancestry back to the Knights of the Round Table, or at least to the Wars of the Roses.

What made it difficult for an observer from such a country to understand the working of a Labour Government was precisely this. One could prove, I imagine, that the incoming Conservative Government has more public school, upper-class members than had the Wilson Government, that while the one is more Oxbridge the other was rather L.S.E., and even, in moderation, T.U.C. But was there a real commitment to create a society in which class would not determine from birth one's education, job, environment, attitudes? Was the New Order still to be founded on hereditary rights and riches, distinctions and privileges? Did people really want to destroy the old order, or in actuality simply to do what had been done in British history before—to take over power and privilege, not through revolution but through peacefully and happily becoming the Establishment?

It would take a keener mind than mine, and a more thorough knowledge of England than I possess, even to try and answer these fascinating questions, since one might well find in the answers a key to the rise and fall of Labour. I was only an ill-prepared observer, and I took back home a mixed bag of observations. I admit, for instance, to never having been able to follow intelligently the endless argument regarding the Common Market, the position of the pound sterling and the evils of an unbalanced and/or balanced budget. On the other hand, I thought Richard Crossman was very principled when he refused to dress up for the State Opening of Parliament, although I did not know how heavily his action contributed to the advancement of Socialism. I thought it odd to hear the band playing tunes from *Fiddler on the Roof* when the Guards changed at the Palace; but on the other hand, why not?

Or, take for that matter, Alf Garnett in the controversial television series *Till Death Us Do Part*. I wouldn't know whether Alf was, sociologically speaking, typical of the

English working-class or not. I was told that the writer intended to make his character the prototype of everything that was reactionary, jingoistic and outmoded in British life and society and because of that a figure of ridicule and fun. But as is well known, the result was rather different. Far from considering him a relic of the past—him and his prejudices *against* 'coloureds,' transplants, permissiveness and *for* Royalty, Churchill and the Empire—millions of faithful viewers couldn't have agreed with him more, actually finding in his sermons the articulation of their own sentiments.

Malcolm Muggeridge, discussing the Alf Garnett phenomenon in one of his articles, pointed out that we—*we*, the enlightened, progressive, forward-looking contemporaries —have our own sets of goodies and baddies, just as in the Westerns. The Vietcong, birth-control, abstract art, psychiatry, demonstrators against apartheid, etc., are all goodies. The Pentagon, the Pope, Greece, etc., are all baddies. Israel, it seems, is a complicated case: when in danger of being annihilated she's a goodie; when she wins a war, she joins the ranks of baddies.

Using these criteria, Alf Garnett is a real baddie. So how could millions of viewers have come to like him to such an extent that it was thought necessary to stop the series? As a foreigner and a declared goodie, I must say that I too liked the old cockney enormously, his views notwithstanding; he was a real person, flesh and blood, and more of a working-class reality than the image conjured up in left-wing weeklies or in the talk of one's own intellectual acquaintances. What was Labour's long-term impact on Alf Garnett and the millions who thought like him?

Something else comes to mind—Enoch Powell's speech of April 22nd, 1968, in Wolverhampton. Many have tried to minimise its importance, but I keep wondering. It was not so much what he said on coloured immigration that shocked me, that it should be stopped forthwith, that Asians, Africans and West Indians at present in Britain should be encouraged to go back where they came from, Commonwealth or no. It was the impressive demonstration of sympathy for his views, the one hundred thousand letters he allegedly received from all over the country, the spontaneous march on Westminster by dockers and other workers anxious to express their support.

Ian Mikardo, one of the leaders of the Labour Left, was a target for the demonstrators. Mikardo had commented on the meaning of Powell's emergence as a spokesman for racialist views. Powell, said he, gave racialism the stamp of approval, coating it with a respectability that would make it acceptable in polite society. Henceforth racialism would be rallied around a standard-bearer who was a scholar, a gentleman and a former member of the Government. Mikardo is M.P. for the cockney kingdom of the London docks—which meant that it was no other than his own constituents who formed the bulk of those marchers in support of Powell's ideas. A delegation granted entry to the House to submit their petition there nearly got involved in a fist-fight with him, and other Members of Parliament found themselves flooded with a spate of threats and protests. Mikardo publicised a letter sent to him from Birmingham—as likely as not from one of Powell's constituents—stating that 'Labour stinks of Jewish scum like you'; it denounced him for having the gall to dare talk about democracy and freedom of speech, and advised him to 'get the hell out of here back to stinking Israel,' with the threat of a bullet in his head if he failed to follow the advice of the sender.

Now, the demonstrators and the letter-writers were, I assume, Alf Garnetts, people who should have belonged to Labour. In real terms, when one considers the numerous measures taken since the war towards the establishment of a Welfare State, Labour did a lot for them. Their hearts and their minds, though, were not in the same place as their stomachs and their purses. The former must have been influenced by other, not necessarily material, factors. The disintegration of the Empire and the total helplessness that descended upon John Bull, wrote the late Kingsley Martin, must have had a psychological effect on the British people. The British working-class was never imperialistic, wrote

Martin, nor did it matter much to them whether the British ruled over India or not. Yet the idea of Britain's decline— not only in world affairs but in sport as well—does play a not inconsiderable role in their sense of national humiliation. It is said that productivity increases in British factories when England wins an international match, and that it decreases in a town whose team has just lost its place in the national league.

Could it not be, then, that having a 'native' from a former British Colony as your next-door neighbour, as your mate in the same factory, that having his children at the same school as your children and his wife shopping in the same supermarket as your wife—that all this adds up to a profound sense of humiliation? Powell wants England green and white, mourning (in *A Nation Not Afraid*) the fact that we no longer have 'a globe with one-quarter of the land surface coloured red,' and that our naval and air predominance, as well as our commercial, industrial and financial primacy have become 'things of the past.' To lose all that and on top of it to find oneself with an Indian, a Pakistani and a Caribbean as one's equals—this must be hard on the Alf Garnetts, and possibly not only on them.

Before coming to the United Kingdom, I never thought of the country seriously as a home of different peoples. I knew, of course, that there was Wales and Scotland and Ireland, but thought this was really past history. It was only when I first visited Edinburgh Castle, and listened to a Scottish guide's version of the bloody battles with the conquering English, that I began to feel the depth of emotion that still existed there. Sometimes the point was made to me half-jokingly, sometimes by way of comparing Israel's revival to the lost hopes of the Welsh and the Scots. But the sentiment was unmistakably there, as we, with our hyper-sensitive Jewish feelings for such matters, never failed to notice. Marx must have been mistaken here too when he thought that class was the proletariat's first real loyalty while Nation was anyway a bourgeois invention.

Now, how were all these undercurrents reflected in the working- -and thinking—of Her Majesty's Socialist Government? Our times will not be remembered as vintage royalty years, but they have not been very favourable to Socialists either. Middle-class is the magic word, and this is perhaps why Harold Wilson laid the emphasis not on class but on consensus, not on a just society but on sound management—as if to invest in Labour was good business.

As mentioned earlier, the ethos of the just society was very central to the attitude of an Israeli like myself. That no such ethos guided Labourite England struck me as inconceivable. Certainly Labour wanted to do, and succeeded in doing, many good things, but they were not the crusaders of a New Jerusalem. They were preoccupied with pragmatics, taking good care not to change the values of the present system. Now and then they would threaten the Lords, but one could not help feeling that many a Labour man would like to spend his retirement in the Lords. People might be moving from one class to another unless they were already titled, wealthy or both, but class as such was still a cornerstone of society. One noticed it almost everywhere, in the formalised rigidity of ceremony, in the way people would collect initials after their names and see to it that they were always mentioned; in the eager translation of money and power to the same old status-symbols so dear to the heart of the Old Establishment; even in the vocabulary, which to the foreign ear sounded very mandarin. Class was the various sections in every pub. It was the different entrances to the theatre. It was the tradesman's entrance found in many houses. (It took us some time to realise that by insisting that tradesmen and caterers use the main entrance to our house we only embarrassed them. They do not *want* to mix, they seemed to be telling us.)

Labour rightly took pride in many of the measures it introduced, and one did not think Barbara Castle exaggerated when she wrote that, under Labour, Britain was entering a period of change and reform for the first time since World War I. But despite all that, one did not feel the cool breeze of the 'air of change.' Labour was convinced it was doing all the good things *for* the people, but was it *by* the people—or was Government one thing and the people another?

In an illuminating article, Paul Johnson, then editor of the *New Statesman,* analysed the Government's psychological difficulties. He pointed out that the very fact that there was a Labour Government represented a challenge not only to the strength and the money of the people to whom the country in fact belongs but also—and more importantly—to their self-esteem. For the people themselves, the British workers, regard is as right and natural for the ruling to be done by the ruling class; having it in the hands of the workers, so to speak, made them feel uneasy. As far as they were concerned (Johnson continued), a Conservative Government, however much it might undermine their interests, was a natural kind of phenomenon—'like rain on Sunday, labour pains or death.' The wealthy, on the other hand, considered a Labour Government to be a kind of violation of the natural order of things where everyone and everything had its place, and royalty, Lloyd's and the pound sterling were facts of life. The Conservative Establishment simply could not accept such a miscarriage of the way things ought to be. For a Tory, a Labour Government was some kind of constitutional misdemeanour, legalised larceny. Johnson concluded that any Labour Government must be prepared for hostility on the part of the rich, and that the latter are bound to activate their power over the press in their own interests. This was true for television, which at best is 'neutral on the side of the *status quo,*' as well. What a Labour Government needed to do, then, was to engage the help of the forces which put it into power—to discard any idea of a consensus and to fight back openly by launching a full-scale and continuous assault on the forces of mammon and of privilege.

What did Labour do to change these centuries-old attitudes? In Israel we have all been too politically-minded, I am afraid, and it has been the firm belief of every party and splinter-group that every party and splinter-group should have its own 'organs,' which also meant a daily newspaper. The *Histadrut* (General Federation of Labour), founded in 1920 with a membership of about 4,000, not only had its own daily, weekly and publishing house, it also worked out its own cultural policies and established a network of progressive, 'labour-orientated' schools. When one thinks of the stamina of those people, one is astounded by their naïve confidence, which bordered on arrogance. How dare they undertake all that (and I have not even mentioned the numerous economic projects of the Histadrut, started in those years—banking, building, transport, marketing, industry, agriculture)? One must conclude that the circumstances were favourable, in the sense that an existing establishment was almost non-existent. And, furthermore, that they were operating under the premise that everything they did was a step towards the realisation of the 'society of the working man,' which was their goal.

This may explain the difficulty I had in understanding Labour's fatalistic dependence on a press that was, by and large, not exactly sympathetic. There was, of course, the trauma of the *Daily Herald* and its death, but the fact remained that even had Labour wanted to project its ideas, its own interpretation of what it did or intended to do, there was no mass media through which the voice of the new society could be heard. What's more, whenever I mentioned the need for 'educating the masses,' brows would immediately be raised. No, a distinguished left-wing leader said to me in the spring of 1968, we cannot even dream of having a daily again. We have lost that battle, and we know that we may be paying heavily for it, come next election.

For a moment there was the impression that the paper Czars were in fact only paper tigers. I refer to the confrontation between Cecil King, chairman of the *Daily Mirror*, and the Prime Minister, which came to the fore in the beginning of 1968 with a news-item disclosing an alleged conspiracy to topple Wilson and install a National Coalition in office. This was the first indication that Labour might be losing its supporter in the mass press, the *Daily Mirror*. This was interesting, since King himself had said on a previous occasion, quoting Lord Northcliffe, his uncle, that newspapers 'could amplify a swing of popular opinion but could do nothing to reverse it.' Accordingly he thought that it was not 'realistic' to credit the *Daily Mirror* 'with winning the election for Labour in 1945.' All it did was to enhance the swing by voicing the feelings of the British public.

But then Cecil King published his leader on the front page of the *Mirror*—on May 10th, 1968—calling for Wilson's resignation and for 'a new beginning under a new leader.' Now, the British—like the Japanese—seem to live on a diet of fish and newspapers. And every second Britisher is a *Mirror* addict. (According to King: 'Our readers tend to be young, with no particular voting loyalties and are more likely to listen to the views of their newspaper than the readers of any other journal.') King had now called to arms his vast armies, declaring war on Her Majesty's Socialist Government. In so doing, did he act in accordance with his uncle's view that the *Mirror* could only enhance the swing (this time back to the Tories)? Or was this the manifestation of a power struggle? If so, the test of power ended unmistakably. Cecil King came to his office only to find out that he was chairman no more. And while spokesmen for the Prime Minister denied any involvement whatsoever in this sudden, mortal blow—the message seemed to be very clear: King was naked of real power—and Harold was king. Paper tigers were just that.

Or were they, one is bound to ask now, in view of Labour's 1970 defeat?

In any event, my aim in this chapter is to hint at some of the things which a foreigner, keen to be witness to Wilson's New Jerusalem, found odd. The list of the Government's achievements was by no means negligible, and not only in financial and economic affairs. The abolition of capital punishment, the new divorce act, a more humane approach to homosexuality, the ambitious plans for reforming the education system, the activities of the Arts Council and the University of the Air idea so dear to Jennie Lee— these were just a few of the things which came to pass under Labour.

And still, as much as one looked for it, one did not discover any genuine popular enthusiasm, any feeling that here was 'our' government, that 'we'—workers, youth, intellectuals—are leading Britain on a new course. Give Caesar his due, and leave it at that. The brain-drain, for instance, was an ever-present indication not only of higher material rewards overseas but of the mood of gloom regarding Britain's future—and in this respect one could not tell who was occupying Whitehall, Tories or Socialists, 'them' or 'us.' It is not enough that the right things are being done, they have to be seen to be right (or left).

My point is that the whole idea of 'Left' and 'Right' has long ceased to be a clear-cut issue, and words have taken on Orwellian meanings in the minds of many people. Were the Young Liberals, for instance, left of the Labour Establishment or right of it? Were not many of the original Welfare State ideas adopted by leading new Conservatives? And is not the real ferment, the negation of the existing system, outside *all* the existing Parliamentary Parties, Labour included? And does the majority of the younger generation truly care for any of the above, the New Left and the Outsiders included?

I must admit that I followed with great interest the renewed outbursts of stories about 'Kim' Philby, who had disappeared in Beirut in January, 1963, and reappeared in the British Press as a major sensation. I imagine that among the many reasons contributing to the outpour of stories on this defected counter-counter-espionage defector, the decisive one was the merciless fight for survival of that peculiar species called Newspapers. Be that as it may, the various Insights helped me too to get an insight into the peculiarities of the Old Boy network, the cement holding together the bricks of the system. With the journalists, the readers, the ex-friends of Philby and his co-defectors, Burgess and Maclean, I wondered: Was it just one of those sordid spy stories, with an overdose of deceit, alcoholism, homosexuality, murderous ruthlessness? Or did all these 'I Was' stories combine into a social novel, whose hero is a person leading a double life—holding a central position in one world while his own centre is in another? In other words, was this just the case of corrupt individuals who had betrayed their country, or did the whole episode reflect the spiritual and ideological crisis of an entire generation?

Last, but not least, can the Philby affair teach us something about the nature of the society that enabled him to lead such a double existence so comfortably for thirty years? Could the fault be in the very principle so sanctified by the Establishment—that what counted most was one's proper background and not one's intrinsic value? Was Philby not enlisted into the holy of holies of a most sensitive security establishment just because he was who he was rather than what he was (or wasn't)? In his cynical way, Philby describes his first contact with the world of intelligence, his mental image of the person he thought would meet him at the select St. James's Club. In all probability he would be a tall, thin man 'with a clipped moustache, talking in clipped sentences and having clipped brains.' In point of fact, it was a woman, but the principle must have been correct. Having had the right background, his colleagues never bothered to go into his curious flirtations with the Nazis (which might even have absolved him of his Leftist sins) or his Communist leanings at Cambridge. *The Observer,* whose correspondent in Beirut Philby had been at the time of his defection, even submitted a sociological apology for this. Where would the Secret Service enlist loyal men if not among people 'we all knew,' at school, socially, within the closely knit club—the Establishment? Even after the defection of Burgess and Maclean (which cast heavy shadows on Philby and had him classified as a security risk) Philby still found his way into a different branch of the Intelligence Service—with *The Observer* job as a cover. The Prime Minister had publicly acquitted Philby of all suspicion, and the Government had privately and informally (according to *The Observer*) approached the distinguished Sunday paper to help him, on humane grounds. His Old Boy approach went, according to *The Sunday Times,* even further. When it had been established beyond doubt that Philby was working for the Russians, a certain man was sent to him in Beirut. A personal friend, of course. Why wasn't he arrested on the spot? How did he manage, after all that, to escape to Moscow?

Who am I to answer these questions raised in the London Press in the late 'sixties? I just wondered whether all that was possible only in Old England, or whether the same Old Boys' system was still at work, the élitist approach still general? Was it just the kind of world in which Sir Henry ('Chipps') Channon could become Private Parliamentary Secretary to Lord Halifax in spite of the fact that he was not interested in sports, business, statistics, Parliamentary debates, speeches, war and the weather (as he admitted in his *Diaries*) but in lust, furniture, glitter, society, jewellery . . .?

Why only him? One reads with great wonder the *Diaries* of Sir Harold Nicholson, and the story of his decision to change horses after the war and run for Parliament as a Labour candidate in a London working-class constituency. Only his determination to enter Parliament—or if honourably defeated to get a lordship as a consolation prize —was stronger than his disinterest in his prospective constituents. He was not elected, but was his candidature such an extraordinary one? Have not others succeeded where he failed?

Now, what have these two very reputable gentlemen, members of clubland and the innermost corridors of power, to do with the Socialist Government of the 'sixties? What has this disreputable member of the Establishment, Philby, to do with it? Nothing, really, except for the disturbing thoughts reading about them provoked in the mind of a foreigner. Philby went to the right public school and the right university, had the right friends and was naturally thought to be fit for the right jobs. He had lots of good luck, and with just a little more of it he could have become the head of the Secret Service. In an élitist class society that seemed as natural as the other side of the same coin—the conviction of the working-class that 'them,' the privileged, the educated, the upper-crust, were ruling by right and that they were the only ones who should and could rule.

John Le Caré, in his brilliant contribution to the book *Philby, the Spy Who Betrayed His Generation,* has interesting things to say about the post-war climate in which Philby operated. While in the last stages of the war it seemed as if the world was accepting some sort of a comfortable, pragmatic, international socialism, with the outbreak of the Cold War people were asked to join a new crusade. While the public mood tended to lean towards the left, as proved by Labour's victory over Churchill, the Intelligence was predominantly rightist. Because of the Cold War, the Attlee Government preferred not to inject new, socialist blood into them. The Services worked under the assumption that one's class is identical to one's loyalties. Philby was the rotten fruit of the crisis years between the two wars, of the aftermath of World War II and of the sudden quenching of the socialist flame.

Maybe. It could be that my lengthy preoccupation with class has to do more with my own Israeli background and my fascination with English forms than with the realities of the Wilson years. *The Observer,* for instance, took the view that the Philby case had nothing to do with the System. A Philby of the future, a product of the comprehensive school, will probably betray as easily his comprehensive school friends. . . .

However . . .

I never missed an opportunity to visit Oxford and Cambridge, to touch the timeless beauty of the cloistered colleges, the ivy, the rivers, the lawns, the sandstone walls, the heavy wooden gates, the air of mystery. In one of these ancient Oxbridge colleges I had the privilege of being invited to have a private lunch with the Master. An arched gateway. A heavy door on its huge iron hinges voicelessly closing behind us. The room is not large, and through the stained-glass windows the delicate spring air is filtered in. Spring is new-born, but the room is in all probability just like it was five hundred springs ago, like it will be after five hundred more winters. The arches, the beams, the old whispering butler in his formal dress—all is beyond time.

My host is not young any more. His tweeds are very neat, his voice soft and slow, only his grey eyes, when the fire is caught in them, reveal something of his adventurous war years. After one gets accustomed to his deceptive tone,

one is carried away by his witty observations, his cultural associations, personal reminiscences, informed views, casual recall of things heard from the great men of our times he had known. We enjoy the food, we empty glasses of excellent French wine, we go over to the fireplace, have coffee, brandy and a cigar. As is usual with me, I feel intoxicated, and not only because of the wine and the brandy and the strong cigar, but this unusual atmosphere and the effort to absorb the compact and clever conversation of the Master. And suddenly, for no reason whatsoever, I mention Philby, voice the same question on the wider implications of the case, on the social structures within which this spy operated for such a long period of time in so sensitive a position.

My host's response is immediate, spontaneous, deeply felt, hurt. I could not have known, of course, that they were both of the same generation, background, schooling. All this talk about the Old Boys' network, he said, is utter nonsense, as is the conclusion that some people want to draw from the case of one odd ball. Why discuss him and see in him a typical product of his generation and background and not see his numerous contemporaries, loyal to their country, holding responsible positions in politics, administration, education, literature, journalism and so forth. Will a destruction of the public school and the select grammar school produce better people ? Will the mass-production university ever equal a system that had given the country an élite which is the envy of the world ? No, said the Master at the end of an extremely illuminating discussion, there is no alternative to this system which condones nothing but the best.

I have often returned in my memory to that spring afternoon in the medieval Oxbridge college. I saw it while sitting in my room, oven-hot, on an Israeli summer's day, looking through my window at the white concrete of the new houses, the parched sands, the still uneasy marriage of ancient history and emergent sociology. I thought of it when I heard of the outcome of the 1970 General Elections and recalled a journalist's observation that the Queen speech in Parliament had reflected the Government's schizophrenia rather than its hypocrisy. This observation may have concealed an even deeper truth, the ambivalence of Labour's attitude to the time-honoured system, the ambivalence of the country's attitude to Labour's plans for revolutionising Britain. It is as difficult to grasp as English grammar, it is like knowing when to use the present perfect or future past, which to the uninitiated seem a contradiction in terms.

We were sitting in front of the fireplace. Spring lit the stained glass and the aroma of firewood and cigars and very old walls filled the room. Now and then the door would open noiselessly and the old butler would suddenly come in, helpful but unobtrusive. My host was reminiscing about his generation in the same way that we would talk about our small group—what is known in Israel as the 'Palmach* Generation' or the '1948 Generation.' But his was a very quiet and considered tone, tight-lipped, unmistakably confident. The wine and the brandy hadn't made me drunk, but my eyelids were heavy and I seemed to be drifting into a time that was not mine. We were observing the present from a distance, passing on it our considered judgement, in the confines of a room from which doubts are excluded—had been five hundred winters ago, will be in five hundred springs to come.

In a piece Philip Toynbee wrote about his former friend, Donald Maclean, he said that he still thought Donald had been a very decent man and in many respects—a good man.

When we parted, my host said of Philby: 'We were good friends. Kim was charming, interesting—and a good man.'

I still have to learn my grammar. Future Past. Present Perfect.

---

* The *Palmach* was the striking fist of the *Hagana*, the underground army of Palestine's Jewish community prior to the establishment of Israel.

One needs to see the black mountains of coal slag in Wales, many of them long since covered over by a fine layer of soil, in turn carpeted by fresh green grass; the stone mining-villages that cluster beneath them—the giant pyramids of the Industrial Revolution and the wretched dwelling-places of its slaves. Then one begins to understand that the Revolution did not just happen.

Experience has taught us that there is nothing like seeing things for oneself. We also know that more than a century has elapsed since the golden age of the said Revolution (counting from the big Crystal Palace Fair of 1851) reached its peak; that more than eighty years have passed since a certain Englishman named Arnold Toynbee (not the one of our times) coined the term 'the Industrial Revolution,' and since a famous Russian, Dostoyevsky, bemoaned the fate of modern society as epitomised by the Crystal Palace in his *Notes from the Underground.* Yet for all that, there is nothing like seeing things for oneself.

Doing so, however, tends to upset all kinds of preconceptions. What historic date marks the revolution which transformed a verdant England and heralded the onset of the machine and city age for the world entire? Scholars attribute it to the first mechanical loom and the invention of a spinning jenny; to the increased use of energy in the operation of machines, first through hydro-energy and later through the steam-engine; to the emergence of the factory—in other words, somewhere between the mid-eighteenth and early nineteenth century. More precisely speaking, it was then that steam-engines were properly perfected and effectively introduced into the coal and iron mines; it was then that fresh power was injected into the 'iron horses' to drag long trains in tow along the railway lines; a new era opened up in shipping, change came to the world. When did it all begin? Two hundred and thirty years ago? One hundred and fifty? A hundred and twenty? Long, long ago.

And it was the English, as we have said, who brought it all upon us. Yet the English, as we have come to know, are a people full of paradox. It was they who built those horrendous cities, who tore at the entrails of the mountains of Wales and the hills of Yorkshire, who laid down railway lines and put up bridges, who covered the face of the heavens with the smoke of chimney-stacks. Yet it is also they who are the greatest lovers of nature—of their own back gardens and vegetable patches, of the public parks and gardens, of the remoter parts to which they make long excursions. There are all kinds of love.

People say that the Englishman considers week-days to be no more than a rather protracted nuisance—the shorter the better, as far as he is concerned. Generally speaking, they have two days of rest—Saturday and Sunday. Anyone that chances upon the City at lunch-hour on a Friday, however, will see for himself the sudden panic which assails all and sundry, everyone fleeing from town as though the Great Fire had started up again. The English get the better of week-days several times a year, moreover, by turning certain Mondays into bank-holidays, when all alike put down their tools, or by having an Easter Monday or a Boxing Day, or by some other device which prolongs the week-end by a day or two. The trains are still trains, but the Automobile Age has hit the United Kingdom, too, and whoever has a car (the really posh have a caravan with beds, kitchenette and all the rest of the paraphernalia that goes with camping out) —gets up and out.

Where do they go?

The privileged few, obviously, make for their country homes, generally less than an hour's drive from town, in one of the Home Counties—and the grander the better. The crowds make for various seaside towns (in the summer and the spring, at all events), there to set up camp with all the rest of the holiday-makers on a stretch of farmland or at the edge of a forest. We found ourselves being caught in the same trap on more than one occasion, part of a traffic jam which stretched as far as Hastings in the south-east. With the thousands, we sought refuge in the bosom of nature, and it took us hours of crawling before we managed to extricate ourselves from the motorised embrace of that same bosom. But once we succeeded in getting out on to a side road, and from there to an even smaller and narrower side road stealing its way between cornfields, copses and orchards, we were not sorry. It was as though industrial England had never been. Beyond a clump of ancient oaks lies a broad green meadow with a large Tudor house at the far end, the black wooden rafters that form its sturdy frame contrasting typically with the gleaming white plaster of its walls. One can tell the house from its sloping roof, its attic windows and chimneys of red brick jutting out on top. The house I'm talking about has an extraordinary Tudor beauty, reconstructed to resemble as closely as possible the home of the sixteenth-century gentleman farmer by whom it was first built; hence the heavy wooden front door, hence the smoky glass and diamond-shaped lattice-work of its windows, hence the heavy wooden furniture cluttering its many rooms. The furniture, needless to say, was not exactly inherited by the present owner of the house from the aforesaid gentleman, a contemporary of Henry VIII. The former bought it up in various antique stores (perhaps on the Portobello Road) or else brought it across from the Continent.

There is a marvellously pastoral air about it all. We have a drink of intoxicating Kentish apple-cider, a speciality of the local farmers. Had we wished, we could have taken a swim in the heated pool, together with the master of the house and his family. We could have (only to us an English spring seems like winter) sent our blood coursing in a sauna imported, plank by plank, all the way from Finland. That is what the other holiday-makers here do. They have taken rooms in a pleasant little flat which the landlord installed in the roundish structure—typical of the region—where they dry the hops used for brewing ale. So there you have the pastoral air, which the landlord is able to sustain simply because he makes his money from the business he does in London—a business which is anything but agricultural.

That is one of the things one can do. But anyone who leaves London at the week-end can see crowds along the highways stopping their cars at the edge of a wood, putting up a table and a few chairs, laying out a meal, pouring tea from Thermos-flasks, sipping away, looking at one another and at the cars passing by, breathing in the scented air, baring a white shoulder to every pallid ray of sunshine, intent on the worship of nature. That is another thing one can do.

He who leaves the city for the seaside and bathing resort can also see the crowds having their fun. Hotels large and small stretch the entire length of the promenade. On the beach itself, on a day we would describe as partly cloudy to overcast, people will be taking a dip or wading out to sea, trouser-bottoms uprolled, when the tide is out, only to retreat to the pier as the tide moves in. If they are not engaged in one of these two enterprises, if they are not sipping their beer or eating fish and chips, one will find them crowding the amusement arcades at the far end of the pier. The big 'casino' where most people go is filled with slot-machines and one-armed bandits, with attendants who change notes into silver, with hundreds of different kinds of games, with family after family, old and young alike. Once we get there, we stroll at our pleasure from one machine to the next, scattering our pennies in delighted anticipation of rapid riches, watching the ocean as it retreats hundreds and hundreds of yards at the ebb, uncovering for a brief space of time the moist sandy expanse beneath it.

The English have been accused of many things. English girls, by way of example, have been accused of lacking both charm and beauty. I know of nothing more unfair. The same goes for the reputedly cold temperament of the English. It is true that a large auditorium full of Englishmen is quieter than a roomful of Israelis, but he who wishes to grasp the English temperament should give a thought to their passion for gambling—whether for bingo, slot machines, roulette, the horses, or whatever. One evening I was taken to see a dog-race, the oddest of all races imaginable: a few greyhounds chasing after a mechanical hare for the space of approximately one minute, or less. I could not for the life of me tell one dog from the next. I did not even have a chance to begin identifying the one of my choice; before I knew what was happening, I knew that I had lost. Yet even the dogs are preferable to a betting-shop, where one does not so much as glimpse the horse one puts one's money on. The English apparently spend about a billion pounds sterling a year in the hope of winning the grand prize. How can a person accuse people who believe in such things by day, and in ghosts by night, of being cold fish ?

All this is merely by the way. Let us return to the trip I meant to tell about and have not even begun. . . . The other alternative is to make an extended stay—in true sporting spirit—in the bosom of nature. That is what we ourselves did one August, and thus got to know at first hand some of the enchanted corners of this isle. Awaiting us at the end of the trip was a tasty piece of bait set by friends. They told us they had rented a house on one of the tiny islands which lie about twenty miles across the sea from Land's End—the Isles of Scilly. Come and see us, they said. We can promise you a Grade A time for the price of a Grade Z hotel. The idea intrigued us, and we had nothing to lose. So I went to a place in the East End where they hire out camping equipment and brought back a big tent of the kind that folds up into a neat little roll small enough to fit easily into the boot of our car. We got together sleeping bags, a gas burner, a few bits of clothing, and set out the four of us, on our way. Aware that we were not about to cross either desert wastelands or jungles crawling with wild beasts, we took neither food, quinine nor arms. We were a little concerned about the ever-treacherous weather, but then who thinks seriously about rain in August?

As we had already covered London on our earlier, briefer sorties, we now made straight for the region of the New Forest on the south coast, a little west of the port of Southampton. This vast area, we were told, has been protected since the days of William the Conqueror; nowadays it is used by wanderers like ourselves and—in the parts where it has been deforested—as pasture land for the farmers who have held the right to it since days of yore. We found a bare yet shady patch, and stopped to pitch our tent in a secluded spot beneath the overhanging branches of a clump of trees. We spread out the tarpaulin and began to assemble the aluminium poles which are supposed to keep the tent up. All to no avail. . . . We had got it all wrong, though we knew not how or why. The only thing we did know was that the poles should not be swaying crazily in mid-air, and that the tent-flaps needed to reach down to the ground for us to be able to attach them to the pegs and stick the latter into the damp grassy soil beneath.

The four of us were still busy struggling with our intractable tent when two other cars drove up and parked themselves on the slope of the hump of bald patch above. Their inmates, young families cluttered with small children, jumped out and pitched their capacious tents in a matter of moments. In England, nobody meddles in the next man's affairs unless explicitly invited to do so. We could see that our neighbours could see what we were going through, and they could see that we could see the looks they were giving us. But they waited for us to give them some sign, and we were afraid of making a nuisance of ourselves. Eventually we could contain ourselves no longer, so we asked one of the men if he had any idea of how this strange contraption of ours worked. He and the other men were down there with us in an instant, and with the practised skill of people who are used to doing things with their hands they soon had the aluminium frame up. *Then* they pointed out to us that we had chosen the worst spot imaginable—for where an English August is concerned you need to find a place that is as high up as possible, just in case of unexpected rain. They stayed at the tent until they had it standing straight, with its poles solidly pegged down, they showed us how to pull the flaps down securely, and gave us a lot of other useful advice. Then they went off to their families to get supper ready. From there on our conversations were confined to the exchange of weather forecasts. A man's tent is his castle.

The night we spent in the forest passed pleasantly enough. The few drops of rain which beat down on our tent did not scare us, nor did the rustling of the wind in the treetops. I woke up with a start only three or four times, to the sound of horses' hooves and other unaccountable noises. At first I was sure that some tales of adventure from the Civil War had crept into my dreams, but when I peeked out through the flaps I saw a white horse standing there—right before my nose. I tried to chase him away by hissing and by throwing empty tins (for there was not a stone in sight), but nothing helped. That English horse, and the cows which joined him, were evidently fully cognisant of the terms of the charter granted their master by William the

Conqueror, and they kept on unconcernedly grazing around and about our tent until daybreak.

That morning we set out to visit Salisbury, one of those pretty little towns which England boasts of. Before going into the town and the cathedral for which it is famed, we stopped at two other spots on the way. The first, on the outskirts of the town itself, is the Roman fortress of Old Sarum, which served both the Saxons and the Normans in their time. Then, about eight miles further along the same soft hilly countryside—like a patchwork quilt of green, brown and yellow squares awned by the shadows of dark, heavy clouds scudding above—one comes upon the ancient weird, mystery shrouded megaliths of Stonehenge. We had often seen pictures of them, standing tall and narrow, circle within circle, laid out in a fashion which must have some devotional significance. Yet in that luxuriant setting—where the bustling cathedral of Salisbury was erected some seven hundred and fifty years ago, where the ancient Roman settlement was brought to ruin a thousand or so years ago—the megaliths look as though they had been installed some time last week, transported aboard enormous lorries, possibly in time for a summer festival of sorts. The story scholars tell us, though, is rather different.

Their findings indicate that the stones were transported on wooden logs from the matchless mountains of South-West Wales and thence floated on rafts along the Bay of Bristol as far as the mouth of the Avon at Bristol. From river to river —and by persistent hauling on wooden logs along stretches of dry land between one river and the next—stones were brought to Stonehenge, covering approximately one-tenth of the way on dry land. So arduous and protracted an endeavour must have had some most sublime motivation to impel it. Scholars are agreed that Stonehenge must have been a religious centre of major importance, but no one knows what religion it was, nor what gods or forces of nature were worshiped there. Several features of the place—the megaliths on the outer circumference, the spaces between them as well as the stones standing in the middle and in the column pointing eastward—indicate that the ancients of Stonehenge may have been sun-worshippers. One can draw an imaginary line straight from a given point in the circle, through the stones at its centre (an altar, perhaps?), via the column right to the horizon, to the very spot where the sun rises at dawn on the longest day of the year. Maybe.

One is aware of something further, too. Here at this spot there is also a third Stonehenge, which dates back to the Bronze Age (possibly around the sixteenth century B.C.). Some of the stones were found to have been engraved with daggers and axes, carvings of the sort known only to prehistoric Crete and Greece of the corresponding era. Beads and ornaments with a distinctly Mediterranean character were found in the grave-mounds. What could it mean? Might the Greeks in fact have ventured beyond the Pillars of Hercules? And could there be some connection between them and the Phoenicians who used to voyage to the south-western tip of the island—Cornwall—in order to purchase the tin so abundant there (a fact they concealed with all kinds of fairy tales for fear of the Evil Eye and commercial competition)? Who knows? We are nearing the regions of the Celts, a people rich in imagination and famed for their legends. One persistent tale has it that it was there, between Cornwall and the Isles of Scilly, that the fabled land of riches, Atlantis, long since buried in the deep, was situated. It was there, according to another legend, that a visit was paid by the youthful Jesus of Nazareth, in the company of his uncle, Saint Joseph the silver merchant. Who knows?

My head still whirls from all the many cathedrals I saw in Europe—some so forbidding that one dare not smile within their precincts, like those of Rheims, Rouen, Chartres; the Spanish cathedrals, like the one at Burgos, where an Iberian paganism is still pervasive—in the heavy odour of incense, in the relics of the saints, in the silks and golds and candles, and in the women shrivelled in black, who manifest a devotion not at all unlike the idolatrous awe of their forebears; feathery Renaissance cathedrals of coloured marble, with flowery ornamentation, mosaics, the busts of popes and emperors impaled in stone all around, as at Siena; and the cathedral of Milan, where north meets south, and east west. Salisbury is different. It has no Joan of Arc, or a Hundred Years' War, or a World War I or II, like Rheims, for instance;

nor an Inquisition, like Burgos; no monarchies rising and falling from one day to the next, like Italy. It had no Becket killed at its altar, as at Canterbury; kings did not rule nor Jews burn there, as at York. Why should Salisbury have a cathedral at all?

It was erected in the first half of the thirteenth century —white, decorative, snug. Kings were neither crowned nor buried there, but it is, however, famed as the burial place of several great Crusaders, such as William Longspée the Younger (son of William Longspée the Elder, son of Henry II, half-brother of King John, the first Earl of Salisbury, who is also buried in the cathedral)—who fell in action at Mansoura, while leading English crusaders in battle. . . . The place has magnificent tombstones belonging to the nobles and the worthies of the region for hundreds of years past. The place has that marvellous continuity that is England. For the sake of history and the tourists, a few features of the cathedral which set it apart from others are pointed out to us: that it has the highest turret of any cathedral in England, that it houses (we saw it with our own eyes) one of the four original copies of the Magna Carta, and that it was the place where the regulations governing all of the ecclesiastical districts of the country were first formulated. That's it.

Not far from there, stretching south-westwards to the sea, lies Dorset, the home county of Thomas Hardy. An unforgettable sunset on an endless August day. We drive along, and the sunset travels with us hour after hour, its light filtering through the clouds gathering on the horizon. The sea appears and disappears behind the open hills. All around are hedged patches of field. And there, on the slope of a nearby hill, beyond a field already harvested, beyond a fenced-in meadow dotted with grazing cows, lost among the shadows cast by the trees around, beneath the fleeting shadow of a black cloud—a house. A square farmhouse, perhaps of blackened sandstone, a roof of black tiles turned green. And further on, beyond so many hilly curves and so many greeny patches, another house, a few more trees, remnants of the ancient forest, more sea suddenly ensnaring the setting sun. Where has all the Industrial Revolution gone?

Down to the seashore, with ever more bays and inlets, seaside resort towns that once were fishing villages, huge caravan parks. But first of all, to Exeter, capital of Devon. Quite a few Israelis are convinced that the town is the scholastic centre of all England. Why on earth ? Well, because of an institute for the teaching of English to foreigners, whose fame has reached as far as Israel. At all events, anyone who does get to Exeter need have no regrets, for if he loses interest in this little village of a town he can always do as we did and go straight on. He'll take with him the sight of its cathedral (another one !), of its stained-glass shop which is named after Sir Francis Drake and which claims to have been founded in 1540, and of Mols coffee-shop, which claims to have been founded in 1596. If he has any doubts, he can see the coat of mail of that great sea-hero, and that of another son of Devon, Sir Walter Raleigh. The connection that these two have with Exeter of all places is not quite clear to me, but it is true that from Exeter on to beyond Plymouth the coast of Devon is full of natural harbours merging into the open sea ; and it is no accident that this region produced the great wayfarers of Britain, the seamen who discovered the New World, defeated the Spanish Armada, gave the British Crown its first colony, Virginia. It was from Plymouth that the Pilgrim Fathers set out for New England, to land at a place to which they gave the name of Plymouth, and to become the founding fathers of America.

As on the two previous nights of our trip, this time, too, we started looking for a place to pitch our tent. The clouds which had imparted to the sunset such an unforgettable loveliness seemed loath to leave. A cold drizzle started up and stopped. We did a quick reckoning : common sense bade us hurry on to the nearest town in search of one of the 'Bed and Breakfast' signs hung out by the inhabitants of every touring and resort area in the country. The honour of all four of us weighed heavily on the other side: we had spent good money on renting a tent, had set ourselves up for camping out—we could hardly flee from a few drops of mere water, could we ? We noticed a farmhouse, with a 'Camping' sign on a high post at the end of the curved path leading up to it. For a mere five shillings we were allowed to set up camp in the field, alongside a score of other families already busily getting supper ready, either inside of their roomy caravans or, like us, outside in the open. Less than ten minutes had passed and our tent was up, our gas-burner going, our tinned food cooking—and rain dripping down. We suddenly understood the story about the man who jumped into the water so as not to get wet.

We finished supper and then, seeing that the rain had not stopped, we fastened the tent securely and all climbed into the car and set off for a tour of Plymouth by night. Not in order to see anything, but in order to do something. The people of Plymouth, seeing the rain, had evidently all gone home, and we roamed from street to street making a thorough study of the town's architecture as well as of the one-way system of its streets. Luckily we found a fish-and-chips shop, whose owners must have evidently been suffering from insomnia. We sat there in the car, spread out the newspapers which are wrapped around the wrapping on the fish and chips, having a real good English time. Ordinary English rain is different from an Israeli shower. The same amount of water is spread over England in tiny drops which —in utter defiance of Newton's well-known law—fall more slowly, somehow, with a gentle drizzle often forming a bridge between one downpour and the next. Still, the fish and chips not only warmed out insides, we were so intent on eating them that they helped to pass the time. When I wiped the steam off the windshield, I saw that the illuminated air of the street had been wiped of rain. We rushed back towards our camping site which, to our amazement, we somehow managed to find in the dark. The tent was still standing, and we all crawled in, zipped up the outer and then the inner flaps securely, crawled into our sleeping bags, and hoped for the best.

I don't know how much later I awoke, but it was the rain beating down on the tarpaulin that awakened me. I felt around me—dry. I felt the flaps—wet. What could I do? I lay there and counted the drops; by my reckoning, the field we were in should have turned into a lake by now. I was afraid to budge, lest I jolt a couple of tent-pegs out of their repose in the rising waters, but on the other hand I was afraid of what was going on outside as well. To cut a long story short: we crawled out, went back in, fell back asleep, woke up again, and the rain went on. The sky did not clear until morning, when it was time to get up. It was a freshly-washed, green, fragrant English morning. The families camping around us were busy with breakfast, and a smell of fried bacon pervaded the fields.

I exchanged weather forecasts with my neighbour and informed him—in reply to his most unexpected query—that we were from Israel. I was certain that on top of all my other troubles I would now be forced to do something about the Israeli image abroad. Instead, my camping partner's eyes lit up and he said:

'Oh, good for you, you people really showed the big boys how to behave. Good for you.'

It was an August morning such as we had never known. Very wet, but good for us.

One should have dwelt on the charm of the villages and hamlets we passed on the way, but I do not forget that our destination was fabled King Arthur's Land's End, the lost Atlantis, the Isles of Scilly. As he moves from Devon, into and through Cornwall's rugged beauty, the traveller begins to feel as though he has crossed a frontier. The English place-names disappear and instead one comes across strange Celtic ones—Polperro, Truro, Marazion, Penzance. The landscape changes and, the further west one travels, the more conspicuous is the granite stone—brown and red and all kinds of greens intertwined with windswept vegetation. There are no large towns in Cornwall, even its major centres are little more than villages. Unlike Devon, the houses of Cornish countrymen are not plastered white, concealed beneath low thatched roofs, but are built of square granite stones, their lines are simple and austere, their roofs of stone or slate. You see the stone everywhere, in the fences around the houses, at the entrance to their villages, in the fields. We travel along the southern coast. Suddenly we come upon a horse-shoe bay, enclosed by towering walls of granite. By now we are driving along a twisting rustic road too narrow for more than one car to pass at a time, unable to see a thing on either side because of the tall hedges that stretch along it on both sides for miles on end. We starting sliding downwards again, towards the sea which has made a deep inroad into the land a little west of the lovely fishing village of Polperro, a spot whose charms another thousand tourists have come to admire, blocking the narrow main road and forcing us to go yet further west, to Polperro itself. We push on, to the narrow south-western tip of the peninsula. The bare, hilly area is dotted with curious ruins: a square edifice of stone, like a miniature fortress or village church, with a round chimney on one side. These are the now dead engine-houses of the tin mines. One theory has it that the Phoenicians used to get their precious metal from this very spot (for do not forget that we are in the Bronze Age, and bronze—as you know—is an alloy of copper and tin). In those days, the tin could be collected from the open fields or from the river-beds, but in the course of time they had to dig deeper and deeper to get at it. The structures we saw there were built in the eighteenth and nineteenth centuries, but Cornwall's tin has since lost much of its commercial value, and all that remains of the good old days are these weird constructions, which go so well with the harsh landscape of the south-west, land of King Arthur.

We have been talking about the Phoenicians with great confidence, as though we had seen them for ourselves. No actual archæological evidence of their having been here has yet been found, but being relatives and neighbours of the Phoenicians the idea appeals to us. They must have been here, we just do not know exactly when. We stop off at Penzance, a little town right at the very end of the British Isles, just a few miles from the point called Land's End. Penzance is the port from which we are due to leave for the Isles of Scilly. The town's main street, extending from the railway station and from the quay, is called 'Market Jew Street'. How did the Jews get to the land's end? We discovered some very strange facts in this connection. It transpires that the richly imaginative Cornish folk saw Jews everywhere. Earlier, we mentioned Jesus and his uncle, the tin merchant, St. Joseph of Arimathea, who, according to legend, anchored at Looe Island, in south-east Cornwall.

Moreover, the old tin works used to be called 'Jews' houses.' Why? Furthermore, a little east of Penzance there is a tiny village called Marazion, a name that no one has ever really succeeded in explaining. In Cornish, 'mara' means a market; if so, might not the place-name 'Zion Market' and the street name 'Market Jew' come from a single source? Another theory goes even further, pointing to the fact that the entire name might be Hebrew in origin: 'mara' may not be from the Cornish word for market, but the powerfully associative Hebrew word 'mara', meaning bitter, cited by Naomi on her return from Moab, when she requests her countrymen to 'Call me not Naomi, call me Mara: for the Almighty hath dealt very bitterly with me,' and also the name of a resting-place of the Israelites in the wilderness, called 'Mara.' According to the latter interpretation, then, the name would mean 'Bitter is the memory of Zion. . . .'

This strange encounter with the history of Israel reminded me of what I heard from the great Hebrew writer, the late S. Y. Agnon, when he stopped in London on his way back from receiving the Nobel Prize for Literature in Stockholm. I was privileged to spend some time in his company while he was in England, and heard any number of stories from him—all of which deserve to be told by someone who could do them justice. Here I shall mention just one comment which he made. We were driving through the streets of London in a rented Austin Princess. Some of the things the chauffeur said (I acted as interpreter) affected Agnon powerfully, and all of a sudden he turned to me and said something along the following lines: 'The great shortcoming of Hebrew literature is that it huddles behind the fireplace of the *Beth Midrash* (house of study). Someone should write a Hebrew novel that does not have a single Jew in it. I don't known if it's within your powers, but if you can, this is the novel you should write.'

Well, I got up and drove as far as land's end. And what do I find there? Marazion.

We parked the car at the quayside in Penzance, and set off for our friends on the Isles of Scilly, twenty miles by sea.

I have seen nothing quite like those tiny isles of granite. They are so very small that if people were allowed to build roads, set up parking lots and install garages for the many travellers of our times, there would be no room left for anything else. Accordingly, there are no cars on the Isles of Scilly. People get about on foot on the islands, and they take a boat to get from one island to another. The next thing is the climate there. All of the south coast of Cornwall has something of the fragrance of southern climes, but the Isles really do have some special aroma of a fairytale land. This is particularly so on the island of Tresco, where our friends Sonia and Louis—thanks to whom we actually got there—had taken a house. All one can see from its windows is the wide open sea, the neighbouring island of Bryher, and the islets and rocks which appear and disappear twice a day, exposed at low tide and covered over at high tide. Ten minutes' walk away, in the heart of the island, is the wonderful sub-tropical garden of its masters—the Dorrien Smiths—with its palms and bananas, citrus and yucca and ginger trees, and vast masses of flowers—narcissi, daffodils, violets, irises—for marketing to London.

Some say the Isles of Scilly are the Fortunate Islands which, in Greek mythology, are said to lie beyond the Pillars of Hercules. Here lie the Elysian Fields, the Hesperides, lost Atlantis, buried in the deep. This curious association stems no doubt from the Celtic legend of Avalon, island of the happy otherworld, where the heroes of yore found eternal peace. Legend has it that between Land's End and the Isles of Scilly once stretched the Kingdom of Lyonesse, long since sunk full forty fathoms under sea with all its hundred and twenty fecund villages. It was here (as well as to hundreds of other spots, according to legend) that the Knights of the Round Table fled after the death of King Arthur, until the earth sank beneath the feet of their pursuers, and they all descended to the deep.

It is no simple matter. We did the trip in three hours, crossing in a large and sturdy boat called the Scillonian, yet even though it was a pleasant summery day half the passengers on board were horribly sick. Imagine a trip like that in mythological times. The legend is undoubtedly related to the fact that these islands lie on the sea route which leads to the southern coast of England, and that their whereabouts are doomed to maritime disasters. Those same quite real, not at all mythological inhabitants of the isles used for hundreds of years to make a living from the plunder of ships wrecked thereabout, and a careful record is kept of all vessels which found their end on one of the hundred and fifty islands and on these same cliffs and headlands. A glossy brochure provides an obituary for all 174 different ships wrecked at the Isles of Scilly since the early nineteenth century. Many of the grand figures which used to decorate the prows of such ships are now on display for all to see in the Smith garden on Tresco Island, in eternal memoriam.

At all events, we disembarked safely at the port of Hugh Town, the largest settlement on St. Mary's, and transferred directly to a small steamboat heading for Tresco or, if you prefer, the Smiths' island. Next to the wharf there is one small shop, and a little further on a handful of houses including, of course, the inevitable local pub. Beyond the hill, mainly hedged flower gardens, and the island's other beach, where there is a modern hotel. That is all on the northern, narrower half of Tresco. The rest of the island consists of the Smith property, marvellous gardens with a square stone castle in the middle, a Union Jack flying from its turret.

In actual fact, the family's forebears acquired all the islands by lease at the beginning of the last century, and they were managed by the Smiths until 1920. That year the terms of their lease were altered, and the family was left with only Tresco and the uninhabited islands. Even after we ourselves had joined their realm for the space of a few days, they commanded no more than two hundred and fifty souls in all.

What can one do there? Escape from civilisation. Sit on the beach, the sea at that time of the year (it did not rain once while we were there) like a peaceful lagoon enclosed by cliffs and islands. Watch the water engulfing most of the black rocks at high tide, watch the sea recede, turning capes and cliffs into a single solid mass. Listen to the blood-curdling shrieks of giant sea-gulls. Do what every Englishman—or so it seems to me—would like to do: sit there all alone at land's end, suck a pipe, have a beer, and say not a single word.

You can go fishing, too. We hired a boat from a local

islander, a man with the look of a Viking about him, an unruly beard covering his weather-beaten face—and sailed out to sea, past Tresco, past 'Hell Bay,' to the point where the only dry land ahead is the eastern coast of the United States. The fisherman told us we were sure to make a good catch there. We went around in a circle for about half an hour, but not a thing tugged at our hooks. We were beginning to lose hope, but our fisherman assured us that we were at a spot that was very rich in fish and that, if only we did not lose patience, we would make a big haul. And sure enough, just as he had said, some mackerel suddenly started snapping at our fishing hooks. Within half an hour there were twenty fine fish lying on the bottom of the boat. Now I began to see why the tough Scilly islanders are so attached to their granite isles: when not plundering ships (which they stopped doing long ago) or growing flowers or looking after tourists (their two major sources of livelihood), they take to sea to fish for mackerel.

We spent several days on those magic isles where time stands still. Everything passes them by, and they remain untouched. The survivors of the Spanish Armada fled there, to the Cornish coast. Charles the Second took refuge there after the Puritan Revolution. Harold Wilson has a modest little house there, on the island of St. Mary's. Perhaps he finds he can think more clearly there sitting in a hidden corner, alone, taciturnly English, watching the never-ending play of the tide's ebb and flow. He may sit and watch the tides, but it is scarcely likely that he contemplates mythology. Or the technological revolution either. Possibly the ebb and flow of the political tide.

We made the rough, twenty-mile crossing once again, over Atlantis, over the Kingdom of Lyonesse of King Arthur and his knights. We saw not a trace of the ship of the great Viking king, Olaf Trygvason, who, on his wanderings—so the saga relates—also reached the Isles of Scilly, where he met a holy soothsayer; and it was here, on these islands, that he and his people entered the fold of Christianity.

We returned to Penzance, dry and ready for more adventure. We drove along the breath-taking cliffs of western Cornwall, through holiday-resort towns teeming with people from London and Bristol and all the rest of England's industrial urbania—gambling at all the casinos, eating fish and chips, listening to the Beatles, the Shadows, the Monkeys. Fabulous Tintagel, King Arthur's castle, stands in ruins atop a cliff, the sea lapping at the sands all around. We drove through the black slag heaps of South Wales, along its green and narrow valleys. We swallowed the poison-gas infested air of Cardiff and Swansea. But the time trickled away relentlessly through the sand-glass. We spent one more night, warm and dry, in a pleasant Welsh village on the grounds of a farmer whose smiling face and cheerful hospitality were well worth the five shillings he refused to take.

From there on we were compelled to make our way more rapidly, and it was only then that we realised how small Great Britain was. We did the whole journey in a single day. The many different scenes we passed, all so remote from one another in time and place, remained with us in memory alone. If only we could have stopped for a good few days in Somerset, all so typically Olde England; if only we could tell about the cathedral town of Wells, of all which may not be there tomorrow, like King Arthur, like the Isles of Scilly, like the mournful Scottish ballad:

" And what wul ye do wi' your towers and your ha,'
    Edward, Edward ?
And what wul ye do wi' your towers and your ha,'
    That were sae fair to see, O ? "
" I'll let theme stand til they down fa,'
    Mither, mither,
I'll let theme stand til they down fa,'
    For here never mair maun I be, O."

We left our hearts in the Isles of Scilly.

FAR FROM WHITECHAPEL,
FAR FROM JERUSALEM

IN AUGUST 1966 the Writers' House in Tel Aviv was the scene of a dialogue between a group of Anglo-Jewish writers and a group of Israeli writers on the general theme of Jewish identity in the Diaspora and in Israel. I was not present, as I had left for London a short time before that not very happy confrontation between my fellow-Israelis and my fellow-Jews. But before long I was to get a taste the lack of a common language, of the diametrically opposite points of view which had characterised that meeting, and which seemed bound to estrange them yet further in the future. It was on an autumn evening in the immense and, to me, still very unfamiliar metropolis, in which one cannot help but feel somehow displaced, in a state of exile both physical and spiritual. The Anglo-Israel Association had arranged a meeting at the National Book League, where the British participants in the said dialogue were to relate their impressions of the Tel Aviv encounter. Dannie Abse, Chaim Bermant, Karen Gershon, Emmanuel Litvinoff and Jacob Sonntag, editor of the JEWISH QUARTERLY, took part, and the whole affair was very elegantly navigated by the chairman of the Association, Mr. Kenneth Lindsay. I sat in the audience, and my gloom gradually gave way to despair.
Why?

The first obstacle to a real dialogue was that those party to it knew so little of each other's literary work, and that the contending parties had clearly different cultural terms of reference. The Israelis tended to interpret Jewish identity in terms of Zionist conviction and personal commitment; their English counterparts saw in such an approach a symptom of Israeli arrogance and an inability to comprehend the who helped refugees. The only English he knew was the word 'Barons,' the name of the firm where he hoped to be given buttons, needles, wool, socks and similar merchandise on credit so that he could then peddle them in the villages of Yorkshire. So he stopped several passers-by and quite simply said 'Barons.' One of the people intercepted by young Marks was himself a wholesaler, and he decided then and there to fill up the young man's pack to the value of five pounds. The wholesaler had a cashier whose name was Tom Spencer. He and Marks were to meet again.

In the said interview, Lord Sieff explained the young immigrant's contribution to modern merchandising in Britain. After a period of peddling, he began to set up stands on market-days based on a simple principle—everything was sold at the same price, and so started the institution of a 'penny bazaar'—which, as is common knowledge, has since grown into a chain of some 250 huge emporia, with an annual turnover estimated in terms of hundreds of millions —a symbol of modern Britain.

I have briefly recounted the story of The Family. But one could tell any number of other success stories over and above those of the most spectacular achievements. One could mention scores of families, not right at the top but none the less extremely well-to-do who, in a matter of two generations, have made it all the way from the East End to the North-West, from Whitechapel and Stepney and Hackney and Clapton and Stamford Hill to Swiss Cottage and Hendon and Edgware and back to St. John's Wood; who have risen from the status of downtrodden penniless refugees to positions of superior economic, professional and public standing. In the early years, the Jewish commmunity consisted largely of thousands of tailors and pedlars, unskilled workers in the clothing and furniture industries, petty shopkeepers. Today, the idea of 'the Jewish community' is associated with the prosperous middle-class, yet at the turn of the century, the Jewish ghetto provided ample material for Beatrice Webb's research into the extremes of poverty. As recently as 1930, there were between six and eight thousand Jewish workers employed in the furniture-making industry; by 1957 their number had dropped to a mere thousand. There were twenty-two Jewish trade unions in London of the early 1900s; all that remains today (if it exists at all by the time this is published) is a dwindling bakers' union. There has, on the other hand, been a considerable increase in the number of independent craftsmen running their own businesses. Some half of the furniture industry in London is said to be Jewish, and the clothing industry is predominantly Jewish, too. Second and third-generation English Jews have tended to move to the professions, primarily to medicine, dentistry, law and accountancy. Gradually the immigrant slums are becoming gilded ghettos.

Of the 450 thousand Jews in Britain, the vast majority live in Greater London, and the majority of *those* in the north-western suburbs of the metropolis. There are also sizeable communities in Manchester (31,500), Leeds (18,000), Glasgow (13,400). But even these 'large' communities are relatively small, which is why so much seems to be known about the career of nearly every Jew who has attained success.

One reads it all in the *Jewish Chronicle*. One meets them all at the various functions held by their numerous organisations. One hears about them from friend and foe alike. They have made names for themselves in trade, industry and finance. They figure prominently in Parliament, and quite a few have a seat in the Lords. There are hundreds of Jews in the universities. Jews are extremely active in publishing, in literature and the arts, in the West End, on television. Considering the fact that at most only one in every hundred Britons can be called a Jew, they have attained a degree of success and acceptance which seems to contradict certain of the claims made earlier in this chapter. To understand this paradox, one needs to examine the notion of 'the Jewish community' rather more closely, see what it really means today, what distinguishes it from a mere collection of individuals about whom we know very little beyond the fact that they were born of Jewish parents and have never undergone conversion.

Underlying the notion 'community' is the century-old Hebrew concept of the *kehilla*—the sum-total of communal members are linked to one another by family ties, social connections and business associations, the Jewish establishment has assumed a closely inter-woven pattern, vigilant over Jewish custom and tradition, strongly attached to the State of Israel.

Well, then, everything is fine, isn't it?

Yes and no. The outsider looking in on it all cannot help feeling that—parallel to all this and in sharp contradistinction to what it all represents—the community is undergoing a process of continuous assimilation; he recognises a trend which up to now was manifest only on the intellectual fringe, but which before long might well develop into a major crisis.

To appreciate what is going on, one needs to bear in mind those peculiar features of British society outlined in the preceding chapters. Britain's is not a pluralistic society composed of a variety of newly-arrived groups of immigrants, each with its own traditions, modes of life, articles of faith. We are talking about Britain, where everyone's position is clearly defined according to his background, family tree, education, clubs, accent. People know their place.

Having survived the first phase of his sojourn in the country, having made that much money in rags, furs, clothing, property, show business—the immigrant takes a well-deserved rest, looks around and asks: And me, where is *my* place?

So he looks for a place outside the immigrant ghetto. He buys a bigger house in a better neighbourhood, yet takes good care there is a synagogue within walking distance of his home. He may not have enjoyed the privilege of a proper education, but for his son he wants the best his money can buy. He'll do anything to get his son into a good grammar school and—if he has really made it—to a prestigious public school. And then, of course, the university. It used to be London or Manchester, but lately it has also been very much Oxbridge, and the right colleges. Somewhere on his way up he will have lost or changed his foreign-sounding name, and now he is looking for his place, his real and rightful place, in the heart of his adopted land.

I cited what Brenner had to say about Whitechapel sixty years ago. Even today the visitor from abroad, invited to the home of a Britisher of relatively recent standing, is likely to find that his hosts have already mastered the finer points of this society whose great love is ritual. They will conform to protocol with regard to invitations, food, conversation, and observe the most subtle distinctions between casual informality and strict formality.

On a higher stratum—and on the solid foundation of material success—one's host will be the owner of a fully-staffed town house and a Tudor or Georgian country house for weekend entertaining. He will donate liberally to worthy causes, be on the board of various charitable and artistic organisations, aspire to a knighthood if not more.

I remember a distinguished politician telling me about a talk he once gave to a Jewish group in the East End. He had asked his audience which language they preferred—English or Yiddish. English, they all cried out, Yiddish we speak ourselves. . . .

Oh, yes, it has been a very rapid and radical change. I recall an evening at the town house of a wealthy industrialist from the Midlands. He himself had once been, as they say, a pioneer in Palestine some half a century ago, and spoke fluent Hebrew. One of the guests had formerly been secretary to a famous Zionist leader, was well versed in Jewish culture and, like his host, was by now highly successful. Another guest—the guest of honour, incidentally—was a national figure, a renowned specialist in his field, head of a rapidly-growing industry based on sophisticated technology, a person of discriminating taste, much involved in assisting cultural and artistic institutions in London. We happened to mention Jewish theatre, and he told me with great charm and slightly tearful sentiment of how he and his friends had in their younger days, while still in the East End, been instrumental in helping out a visiting Jewish theatre which had produced *The Dybbuk*, how they had invited the press, how the *Times* reviewer had behaved, and so forth. The man has reached the top, he has more than one house, is an art collector, titled, yet his eyes shine with a special warmth when he reminisces about his youth.

His children, however, and the children of all the others around the table, have childhood memories which differ very little from those of any of their upper-class contemporaries, have the right kind of accent with no trace of foreignness about it—and must crave for nothing so much as to be totally accepted. They surely believe that their forefathers lived not in the forests of Poland or the steppes of the Ukraine, but that they fought at Hastings, won Trafalgar, conquered India. Once fully Anglicised, there will be nothing to compare with their horses, their roses, their orchids. They will go to the synagogue—if they go at all—in top-hats and tails; they'll wear flannels and tweeds in the country, grow clipped moustaches, may even lose their final Jewish trait—being afraid of dogs. Their town houses will be superbly staffed with the most perfect butlers, the finest French cooks, the best company. And they will go jetting, like everybody in their set, to the Bahamas, the South of France, Morocco. But unlike everybody else, they will also include Israel in their itinerary.

But *their* children? What will their place be?

So much for the thin, but influential, upper crust. One wonders, however, whether further down the ladder the pace of total integration—what we Zionists would label as assimilation—is any slower or less profound. Numerous instances come to mind in this connection. I think of the twice-yearly agitation among my Jewish brethren—on New Year's Day and the Queen's Birthday—when the Honours Lists are published. The Jewish press studies the list with a magnifying glass, purrs with pride when it discovers that a Jewish mayor has been awarded the M.B.E., a Jewish publisher or show-biz tycoon has been knighted, a distinguished lawyer elevated to the peerage. They will not go forth with spear and coat-of-mail to fight for the Queen, they will not be presented with feudal estates for their services. None the less, who can withstand the magic of a title, the satisfaction derived from joining the ranks of the aristocracy, blue-blooded or no. And the community as a whole? Most bask in the glory of their fellow-Jews; a few get their pleasure from the name *not* included in the list. One man's garter is another man's button-hole.

I had intended to confine my comments in this chapter to personal impressions; the generalisations I find myself slipping into are necessarily incomplete and perhaps even biased. I must make it clear, then, that all I can pretend to offer are the observations of an outsider. My only excuse being the claim of the old Yiddish saying that 'a guest for a while sees for a mile.'

When one speaks about Jews in Britain, one refers to those who are willing to identify themselves meaningfully as Jews and to maintain a viable contact with the community. Yet of those who do not belong to a synagogue or any other Jewish organisation, whose children receive no form of Jewish education, and who have excluded themselves from the community—of them we know very little. I met quite a number of the latter, mainly intellectuals, writers, artists, people who have rejected the official community described above. They do not frequent a synagogue in much the same way as non-Jews of similar attitudes and views do not go to church. They reject the Jewish Establishment for the same reasons that make them outsiders to the Establishment in general. In considering the dynamics of the centrifugal forces within the Jewish community, I was of course referring to this group, too—a significant segment of British Jewry which is growing in size as it declines in Jewishness. Economic prosperity, possibilities of rapid anglicisation, the secularisation of the society as a whole, the opening-up of the universities to ever larger portions of the population, heightening opportunities in the liberal professions and for careers in academic spheres and in the arts—all these are factors speeding up this process among British Jews.

It is true, as we have seen, that the Jewish community is a highly organised one—but what about all those who treat their synagogue membership as though it were a life insurance policy which yields its benefits only in heaven? Institutes of Jewish learning do exist—but they are of inferior quality, and they serve but a scant percentage of the children. In point of fact, there are only two major colleges for the training of rabbis, teachers and modern community leaders. Orthodoxy seemingly has complete sway—yet its strength is at the same time a source of weakness: it has very little appeal to the younger generation. Behind the impressive organisational façade the outsider who has a chance to peer inside discovers a reality that is rather depressing.

Consider the education system, said to be a good one. In a book called *Jewish Life in Modern Britain,* one finds an illuminating collection of lectures given at a conference held in London in 1962. It includes a paper on education presented by two highly knowledgeable authorities—Mr. Harold Levy and Dr. Isidore Fishman. Their estimates are: (a) the 5 to 15 age-groups number about fifty-two thousand youngsters; (b) 57% of these are enrolled in full or part-time Jewish schools, while altogether more than 75% receive some form of Jewish education; (c) these include two quite distinct frameworks—day schools and after-school classes, the latter being held twice a week from 5.00 to 6.30 in the afternoon and for three hours on a Sunday morning. The article listed about 8,000 day-school pupils (including ten secondary schools) and some 21,000 attending after-school classes.

Let us consider what lies behind these facts. The average pupil will have four years of after-school Jewish education, with the rate of absenteeism ranging between a third to a half. This means that the child receives in all something like 540 hours of Jewish education, which includes the prayer book, Bible, commentaries, further religious instruction, Jewish history and Hebrew. The typical child would begin such studies at the age of eight and leave when he is twelve. Even if we disregard the general level of such schools and the fact that classes are conducted primarily in English, it is clear that the child cannot get very much out of them. The amount of Jewish—let alone Hebrew—knowledge and the extent to which Jewish values are inculcated are meagre indeed.

That leaves us with the Jewish day-schools, which belong to various different organisations, have different educational philosophies and teaching materials, lack a teaching staff specifically trained to meet their purposes. The best known are the ten Zionist day-schools, a source of justifiable pride to the Zionist Federation. Over 3,000 children attend such schools throughout Britain—yet they, too, will complete their studies there at the age of twelve, assuming that their parents have not already transferred them to a normal grammar school. If we include the very good Jewish Comprehensive

School in Camden Town with its approximately 1,200 pupils, Carmel College and various religious schools, we reach an overall number of 9,000 children in both primary and secondary schooling. In other words, only two out of every fifteen children get this, in itself extremely limited, form of Jewish education.

I had occasion to visit a number of such institutions, to see them at work, talk to teachers, children and parents. There seemed little change for the better, as the basic limitations remained: the tendency of the more prosperous members of the community to send their gifted children to non-Jewish schools; the absence of suitably modern teacher training colleges; the so-called religious approach, with its emphasis on rote-learning of the prayer book rather than on a broad knowledge of the language, history, culture and ideals of the Jewish people. I can only quote the words of one of the Israeli participants in the above-mentioned conference, the late Dr. Sha'ul Esh: '. . . the idea of a secular Jewish education has not even occurred to Anglo-Jewry, and was not even discussed. But we had better note that Jewish religious education is no longer taken for granted, and that it is not the only possible approach to Jewish education. The historical events which have taken place in Jewish life in our generation, events which left such a profound impression on all Jews, are hardly felt in Anglo-Jewish education . . . Is it conceivable that all the progress achieved in the past few years in the teaching of foreign languages will have no impact on the teaching of Hebrew in the diaspora ? . . . Of no less interest is the impression one gets of almost total ignorance as far as recent Jewish history is concerned . . . Is it conceivable that some slight acquaintance with Montefiore, Bialik and Herzl substitute adequately for a knowledge of the basic facts to do with the resettlement of the Land of Israel and the establishment of the State of Israel and the radical upheavals in the fate of the Jewish people throughout the world ? '

I have naught to add to these harsh words which, to our regret, have not as yet become outdated.

The point is not that the young have such a poor Jewish education, but that this is the state of affairs in a community

THE JEWS OF MAY AND JUNE

ALL THROUGH the winter the days had been shrunken, grey, frost-bitten, mashed between long nights, but now they were growing, gnawing away mouthfuls of darkness to the left and right of them. The English are a race of flower-worshippers, they plan their public parks and private gardens in such a way that not a single day of spring or summer passes without some new bud blooming. In the North-West, where we lived, one did not need to leave the city to be intoxicated by the sight of nature's resurrection. I would drive past it all twice a day, taking the children to their Camden Town school, along North End Road, by the edge of Hampstead Heath, passing the pond and crossing Hampstead into the dreary Camden Road area—only to come upon yet another of one of London's marvels, this time Regent's Park, before edging my way through the morning traffic up to the point where Hyde Park followed on the left. Finally I would end up in the exclusive tree-lined street with gates sentinelled by ancient green top-hatted guards: Palace Green—shared, inter alia, by the Embassies of the USSR, the Hashemite Kingdom of Jordan, and Israel. No avenue in London is greener, nowhere does one actually see the foliage sprouting out of the bare black branches as on our Embassy Row.

We Israelis never could get used to these dramatic changes, so different from our own country's two quite clear-cut seasons—its winter rainy, green and cool, its summer dry, parched and hot. In London during those spring days of 1967, our reaction to it all was almost physical. Endless talking dried out our tongues, incessant smiling brought on a crick in the neck, we could not tolerate the look of our dark suits. We felt driven by a blind desire to get into the car and drive away—the further the better. Just for a while, to no longer represent, to be simply our own selves.

So we took two week-ends off with a week's holiday in between and crossed the Channel, leaving everything behind but one official thought : we must be back by May 1st in time to welcome the Tel Aviv Chamber Theatre, due to appear at the Aldwych in the World Theatre Season. And indeed, we made it back to Dover right on time, past the intoxicating orchards of Kent then in full bloom, luxuriating in the rolling hills of the South-East, taking a peek at Canterbury, swarming into a metropolis more beautiful than ever in the late afternoon, on the eve of May Day. Back into the starch, we welcomed the theatre, entertained some and were entertained by others, plunged into the same perpetual motion—from one meeting to the next, from this charming person to that very-important personage, to being the epitome of good manners, to constant consultation of a crowded diary.

Those were the days of economic recession in Israel. People discussed unemployment, even the Anglo-Jewish press carried numerous stories about inter-party tensions in Jerusalem. People discussed everything, except for what was only a fortnight away. In accordance with local custom, my secretary would have my schedule arranged weeks ahead, and the bizarre story is still there in my diary : I visited a couple of universities, lunched with a publisher and a cartoonist who was working on a book on Israel ; I courted an up-and-coming publisher who planned (and planned, and planned and is still planning) to publish a series of Israeli novels ; I was to call on my opposite numbers in two or three other embassies. It is all there in my diary except for one item—the fact that the day after Independence Day, that lovely month of May was to turn into the darkest since Israel won its independence.

Events were moving rapidly, and at that distance, thousands of miles from home, everything appeared both much smaller and vastly bigger. We were an Israeli enclave, and supposed to be well informed. Yet we existed in a different context, facing the television screen. Cairo went hysterical, right before our eyes. Military convoys were moving into Sinai. In the Gaza Strip—and in Jerusalem—Ahmed Shukeiry was letting forth his venom, promising to throw us all into the sea. Mobs flourished guns for the camera-eye in hair-raising close-ups. A Syrian Minister interviewed on a news programme states in calm confidence that there is only one solution—the liquidation of the State of Israel. We see U.N. Emergency Force staff taking down their flags and watch Egyptian soldiers moving in. All on television, deadly alive.

At first things looked unreal. On May 19th the President of Israel stopped at Heathrow Airport on his way to Canada to inaugurate the Israeli pavilion at Expo '67. The Ambassador and other members of the embassy were there together with leaders of the Jewish community to welcome him at the airport. I remember the scene very vividly—the worried exchanges between the Ambassador and a senior army officer who happened to be there, too, on his way from one place to another. I recall the confident responses of the President to reporters' inquiries. The very fact of his continuing his trip seems, for a while, to be an encouraging sign. But the omens are bad. George Brown, then Britain's Foreign Secretary, about to leave for an official visit to Moscow, cancels his trip in view of the crisis. There are endless signs that everything that has happened so far is merely the beginning. Hearing the reactions of people considered to be friends, one cannot help feeling that they are more concerned about what we are going to do than about what is going to be done to us. The first warning note is an unequivocal French statement that the Three-Power Declaration of 1950 regarding the safeguarding of peace in the region is no longer considered binding. It is a bad sign, although the declaration had had little meaning even in the good pre-'67 days. Soon after, the Egyptians declare the Straits of Tiran to be Arab waters, and hence closed to Israeli shipping en route to the port of Eilat. Soon the air becomes repugnant with the smell of a new Munich. Never shall I forget those days in London, and the realisation that came with them of what it meant to be a small nation dependent on the goodwill of foreign powers who regard you as a bloody nuisance. The arguments of those who tried to minimise the implications of Egypt's overtly belligerent act proliferated; some went into the question of Israel's legal standing, and suggested that the issue be brought before the International Court at The Hague; others said that even though Israel had a right to cross the Straits, she had never really exercised it to any great extent: *The Observer* carried a front-page feature to the effect that Israeli ships hadn't been there for quite a long time. It all led up to the conclusion that Israel would do best to rely on some sort of 'Community of Nations,' possibly the 'Maritime Powers,' to do the job. One ear was deafened by the war cries of the Arab countries, busy signing treaties and moving troops with the declared intent of waging their final war; the other ear could barely pick up a few feeble voices whispering something about 'Israel's right to exist.' At first things looked unreal, but by the week's end we all felt that time was running out, that all the glib talk about what the International Community would do was an invitation to disaster.

The most meaningful event of that week was the profound tremor which shook—to risk a sweeping statement—every single Jew.

Can one pin-point the day on which that tremor broke the Jewish heart? I see it culminating in an interview with the King of Saudian desertland and oil, at Claridge's, witnessed by millions of television viewers. The King, speaking through an interpreter, stated that the only solution was the extermination of the State of Israel. His words were linked in the minds of many with Nazi terminology, the 'final solution'—a euphemism for extermination—meaning exactly that. People watching *24 Hours* saw a documentary about one of the death camps (Treblinka, I believe), narrated by one of the few survivors. The camera followed the man to the camp, to the mock railway station, to where the actual murder of hundreds of thousands had taken place.

That one word, 'extermination,' was to trigger off an entire chain of reactions. Memories and anxieties stored in the dark cellars of the Jewish collective consciousness broke loose, masks of confidence and security behind which the post-war generation had hidden its real face shattered to bits. That is the only possible explanation for the sudden eruption of emotion. No surviving Jew, regardless of whether he had experienced the horrors of the holocaust in person or not, can ever forget that trauma—the reduction of every Jew to the status of a mad dog, to be shot on sight in full daylight, with all the world as bystanders. In order to mobilise the necessary powers to restore themselves to life and rejoin a 'sane' humanity, they had had (had not we all?) to repress the unforgettable, to lock it in the farthest chambers of their souls. What had been had been, but on another planet. This one (Britain, where our own impressions are concerned) is a world apart, where everything is just perfect, where we have already integrated, where we are it—Tom, Dick and Harry. Certainly, there is the State of Israel, no need to tell us what a great and wonderful country it is, we shall stop at nothing to do our bit for it, if only we can. Is not every single one of us—in fact— an ardent Zionist when you come to think of it? But, my dear sir, things are not, don't you know, as simple as all that.

(Don't I know? Here is the distinguished guest of honour, a Minister of the Crown from Scotland or from Wales, who with great eloquence compares 'my people' to 'your people,' and proposes a toast to 'your President, to your brave people and admirable country—to the State of Israel'—and here are all those proud Zionist faces suddenly dropping at the sound of the first 'your.' . . . And rightly so, my dear sir.)

And then, so unexpectedly—on television—the hawkish profile of the Arab king, against the backdrop of the finest hotel in London, and his explicitly proposing extermination of the State of Israel as the sole solution. The King is not charged with intending to commit genocide. He is not even asked to evacuate his elegant suite. Nothing of the sort. One must always give the other fellow a chance, keep to the rules of fair play. And in the meanwhile—Nasser sits surrounded by the pick of his pilots, in a Sinai air-base, and smilingly invites Israel's Chief of Staff, General Rabin, to try and open up the Tiran Straits if he can. 'Ahlan Wasahlan' goes the ironic invitation. The rhythmic cries of a Jihad rock our television set. By now the vague talk of possible action by the Maritime Powers has been emptied of any real content, if indeed there ever was anything to it all. One begins to appreciate how dire is Israel's isolation, an isolation only underscored by Mr. Eban's intercontinental travels. Israel is looked upon as incurably ill, an unfortunate human exploit which can have but one fate. I'm terribly sorry, people's eyes seem to be saying when they're not avoiding yours, but what can I do. . . .

Extermination: perhaps it did not happen at that actual moment, but the fact is that all that had been locked away in the deep-down recesses of the Jewish soul burst through into the fore of the Jewish consciousness. Never will there be another Auschwitz. The liquidation of Israel will not, of course, entail the physical annihilation of all Jews everywhere, but it does mean that not only shall we regress to what we were before the Jewish State—in the long run the blow will prove fatal to every single one of us.

Be that as it may, we suddenly found ourselves engulfed by a completely unfamiliar Jewish being—moved to the core, identifying with us to the extent of dropping the distinction between 'you' (Israelis) and 'us' (British Jews), and talking excitedly about 'us' (Jews) and 'them' (Gentiles). Not being prophets, we cannot say what Jewish existence will look like in the years to come; but any person who had the good fortune to be a witness to the days of May and June must be convinced that the Franco-Jewish sociologist, George Friedmann, was somewhat hasty in his predictions about 'the death of the Jewish people.' And in this respect there is little difference between the publicly-known-as-a-Zionist kind of Jew and the one whom no one had ever suspected of even being Jewish.

One should note, moreover, that Jewish reaction in Britain was not at odds with the general public's attitudes. One could quote opinion polls, but that is unnecessary. Almost everybody supported Israel, virtually none approved of Egypt's bellicose moves. The British instinctively recalled

Dunkirk, and the blitz, and the Nazis' attempted blockade. I would say that the memory of the holocaust had an effect not on Jews alone. The collective memory of Christian Europe carries all that it has committed against the Jews: the burning of the Jews of York in the twelfth century, the Spanish Inquisition with its fires, the Crusades, the Black Plague, the massacre of entire communities during the Cossack uprising of the seventeenth century, the status of the Jew throughout the centuries as a person without rights, on sufferance—all this preceded Auschwitz, and few are the Europeans who do not harbour somewhere in the darkest corners of their soul the grim knowledge that no European, no Christian can say: I am innocent. It is hard to distinguish, in this context, between the guilty and those haunted by a sense of guilt. There can be small doubt, however, that in so far as the world's conscience was stirred in May of 1967, the thousand-year-old collective memory had much to do with it.

As the drum-beats of the Jihad grew stronger, our Embassy was literally swamped by letters, cables, phone-calls, contributions, inquiries by people wanting to volunteer for active service, expressions of willingness to take 'evacuated children.' During those few weeks the Embassy received thousands of such letters, many of them moving documents which could make an extraordinary book. We wanted to have at least a selection of the letters published as soon as possible. The poet and editor, Jeremy Robson, who in those days devoted so much of his time to Israel, took it upon himself to compile a representative selection of those thousands of letters, and the result was published on Israel's Independence Day of 1968 (by Vallentine, Mitchell) as a small book entitled *Letters to Israel, Summer 1967*. To illustrate the atmosphere of those unforgettable days, I quote a few passages.

Writes an Australian-born psychiatrist holding a lectureship at a London teaching hospital, on May 24: 'My admiration for Israel's great achievements leads me to volunteer my services in any capacity you may think fit. . . . I would be happy to help in any way possible, including serving in Israel's armed forces.'

Writes a State-registered nurse, on May 26: 'I am not a Jew but an Irish Roman Catholic, and feel you need all the help you can get with the Arabs "ganging up" on you as they are. In the meantime, I hope the U.N. can do something to prevent the possible war; if not, then perhaps you would kindly forward my name and address to the department concerned with volunteers.'

Writes the Society for Distributing the Holy Scriptures to the Jews, on May 31: 'On behalf of the Council of the Society, also a large number of Christian people whom we represent, we desire to express sympathy in this day of crisis concerning the State of Israel and to assure you of prayer on its behalf. . . . We would like, if we may, to quote the following passages from the Bible concerning Israel, which we believe will be a help to the Nation, viz.: Isaiah ch. 54, v. 17. "No weapon that is formed against thee shall prosper; and every tongue that shall rise against thee in judgement thou shalt condemn." Psalm 122 v. 6: "Pray for the peace of Jerusalem, they shall prosper that love thee."'

On May 31 'a middle-aged optician with a young family,' writes: 'I am well aware that, individually . . . I would be as much use to you as a hole in the head. I propose to lead a convoy of cars and trucks to Israel. I am convinced this would gather money, men and materials right from Glasgow to Marseilles. . . .'

On June 3, an original offer came from someone 'not of the Jewish faith—being Church of England': 'I feel strongly enough about the transgression by the U.A.R. against Israel to do something to help, namely my working in Israel. Since I have an agricultural education, and experience of poultry farming, I feel I could be of some use in this field, or in any other work I may be required to undertake. . . .'

Particularly moving were the many approaches by people expressing their readiness to receive evacuated children. Such offers would make me shudder, and my reaction tended to be arrogant—under no circumstances will children be evacuated, was the spontaneous reply of us all.

I recall a conversation over the telephone with a lady

I have recounted this conversation in order to illustrate a general attitude. People who found it hard to understand the change of heart which followed Israel's dramatic victory and the subsequent growing anti-Israel sentiment should bear in mind dogmatic adversaries of this sort—to whose credit one can say only this: *they* stuck to their views, in days of despair no less than in days of victory. And despair we did in those days. A friend and colleague of mine, the poet Hayim Guri, wrote in the Tel Aviv daily *Lamerhav* on May 26: 'The people who live in Israel have had bitter experience, and they harbour no illusions; they know that only he who fights wins allies, whereas the timid get nothing but compassion. Action now is a reminder to one and all that in this part of the world no final account can be drawn up that will not include us. A nation determined to live wins life, no matter how costly the price. And so these terribly complex considerations lead to a terribly simple conclusion: We can either act at the right moment, or face defeat.'

In London, I must say, just such a feeling overtook all Jews, the rich and the poor, committed Zionists and the totally assimilated, simple-minded businessmen and sophisticated writers, scholars, artists.

First, the contributions to the Emergency Appeal. There are the regular donators, the big, the small and the medium, whose names are read out at the annual dinners held at the Dorchester or Grosvenor House as well as at many other public and private functions the country over. In those days, however, people did not have to be coaxed or flattered into giving. Many who had never given a penny, whose very existence was unknown, forced their contributions upon us. Impoverished widows sent ten-shilling notes, while people who had formerly contributed thousands doubled and tripled their share. To be quite frank, it was not the 'haves' who moved us to tears, it was the have-nots.

I still see the odd, shabby, stooped man who rang the Embassy bell one morning, carrying a cardboard box tied with pieces of rope, saying he wished to hand it to the Ambassador. It goes without saying that we were very much on the alert in those days, and the man and his box looked rather suspicious. So he was asked to wait in the hall while the receptionist called our administration officer down. By the time the latter came, the man had gone off without anybody noticing. Only the box was left. Taking every precaution, they undid the box. It was crammed with money—new notes, old notes, some greasy, some weather-worn—hundreds and hundreds of them. With all the stories of bank and train robberies, the box looked even more suspicious. Who was the man? Was the money 'hot'? Was it forged? The box was handed over to the Emergency Appeal, and they sent it to the Bank of England to be checked. In a day or two the Bank informed the Appeal that it was all good, honest cash, over £8,000 of it. Who was that mysterious man, stooped, shabby, odd-looking? Were they his life's savings? What had made him hand all that money over? We never learned. The man had emerged for a moment from his anonymity, only to disappear back into it again.

Then there was a group of taxi-drivers who insisted in giving us the meagre proceeds of their mutual-aid fund, who organised a free-of-charge, 24-hour-a-day service in front of the Embassy, insisted on their right to do this 'little something' for Israel. Even after it was all over and the cease-fire had gone into effect, they refused to go away, had to be persuaded to go back to their normal work.

I can see it all as if it were today—the total, overwhelming excitement, everyone involved, each breaking into the other's strictly defined domain. All the ordinary barriers fall. Jewish ladies serve as messengers and tea-brewers. Young Israeli students swarm the Embassy, begging to be sent home on the first plane available. Specialist physicians offer their services to the army, celebrated professors phone through from Cambridge, Manchester and Leeds, ready to volunteer for anything: one had been an officer in the last war, another would teach in any school we liked, a third was prepared to do any kind of work on a kibbutz. Some one had scarcely made mention of the fact that blankets might be needed—a women's organisation reports that they already have on hand 40,000 blankets. Anyone who happened to pass the offices of the Jewish Agency in Lower Regent Street would see long lines of young people, long-haired and mini-skirted, wanting to volunteer for 'anything' in Israel; there were over 8,000 of them within just a couple of days. Enterprising young Israelis don't wait for a seat on a plane—they go off to Paris, Zurich or Athens in the hope that they will be luckier there. A petition signed by Jewish students is handed in at Downing Street, exhorting the Government to stand by Israel. Thousands of cars carry stickers saying 'We stand by Israel' (and a timely joke is born: They say that in Tel Aviv the stickers read 'We stand by Golders Green'). Our people at the Defence Mission work like mad by day and by night, but I see the faces of my friends, senior officers, cursing their bad luck for not being where their true place now is.

The little spy in the back of my head observes, records, finds it all unbelievable, while I, in my own little corner, find myself immersed in activities I never thought would fall my way, catch my old 'connections' knocking at my door, urging me to do something, robbing me of all initiative, desperately demanding: What shall we do? How? And why not sooner, today, yesterday?

In the preceding chapter I mentioned the Writers' Dialogue held in Tel Aviv in the summer of 1966. What they had to say had not made me very happy, since I had felt there was an invisible but very real wall keeping us apart. In the six months or so after our arrival, we came to know more and more of the Anglo-Jewish intelligentsia—prudent professors, writers suspicious of anything that might be Establishment, show-business people, newspapermen, Friends of Israel's universities, museums, orchestras, theatres, kibbutzim, Youth Aliya and what have you, people so removed from the life of the old-style Jewish community that even membership of the Anglo-Israel Association seemed too much of a commitment for them. We used to meet in drawing-rooms, at cocktail parties, at bohemian get-togethers, on the whole very reserved, very polite, trying to reach one another the way hedgehogs do—with the utmost caution. The job I had on my hands was not an easy one, oh no.

We made some very warm friends. One of them, the novelist Gerda Charles, had just been on a first visit to Israel, where she had wanted to get to know Israeli intellectuals. She spent Passover there, and came back the day after Independence Day. Miss Charles is in certain very significant ways different from the ordinary run of Jewish intellectuals whom we have tended to somewhat stereotype. She is Orthodox, and her views on various subjects struck me as a brave dissent from 'progressiveness at any price.' She impressed me as having an extremely sharp eye and wit. Gerda had more than once wanted to go to Israel, yet she had put off her visits time and again, as though afraid of a direct confrontation with the realities of Israel. We met her immediately after her return, and her enthusiasm was obvious. As we had arranged to get together again very soon—at a party we were planning to give—I thought I had better keep the many questions I wanted to ask her till then.

The party never materialised. The situation was deteriorating, and we were too pre-occupied with it to be in a party-throwing mood. On the other hand, we stuck very stubbornly to the principle of 'business as usual.' Having already invited people, we decided to go on with the party. Then Gerda Charles phoned me one day, deeply concerned about Israel, and asked that I postpone the party. Rather let us get together and discuss what could be done to make the world aware of what Nasser had in mind. How can one just sit back quietly with Israel faced with the threat of annihilation? The telephone conversation with Gerda Charles and those that followed with Louis Marks and Dannie Abse and Emmanuel Litvinoff were the turning-point for me. In those days we experienced the frustration of being suddenly deserted by so-called friends. All of a sudden people were not available, or they would look at you as though you were suffering from some incurable disease, to be mourned, not helped. In those days we also rediscovered the Jews, all of them, including that very special brand—the Jews of May and June.

One evening Gerda Charles asked a group of Anglo-Jewish writers to her home. The impression they gave me on that occasion was that they were as worried and as anxious to do anything in their power as were Gerda herself, Louis, Mannie and Dannie. The group included Wolf Mankowitz, Bernard Kops, Chaim Bermant, Lewis Griefer, Lionel Davidson, Denis Norden, Frederic Raphael and Jeremy Robson. The frequent meetings we were to hold from that evening on tend to merge. But I do remember very clearly the mood of that initial gathering, and the letter which was composed on the spot, stressing that Israel, 'a country the size of Wales,' was being threatened with another Auschwitz. Frederic Raphael volunteered to submit the letter to the *Sunday Times,* once a large number of other writers had been asked to subscribe their names to it as well.

The letter came up again at a further meeting held a day later, on June 1st. There was another distinguished participant on that occasion, Mr. George Steiner. He had called on me at my office, saying that he was doing so at the suggestion of a mutual acquaintance. At that moment of grave danger, said Steiner, he felt it was Man's duty to stand by Israel. I said that it seemed to me that the most important help a person of his intellectual and moral stature could render was to let his views be widely known. His reply was that for him it was a question of personal commitment. He wanted to volunteer for work in Israel. He could not volunteer for active service, owing to a physical disability, but he would be willing to teach or do any other necessary work. I was deeply moved and impressed when he said that people should demonstrate their solidarity in some concrete way, even if all they could do was sit in a coffee-house on Tel Aviv's Dizengoff Street. Since I already knew of the meeting that was to take place at Gerda's home that evening (June 1st) with writers and representatives of another group of intellectuals, I suggested that he join us there—and so he did, coming down from Cambridge as speedily as he could.

That was when the letter was finalised. Frederic Raphael said that he had a letter in the *Sunday Times,* and he would ask that his letter be taken out and the writers' appeal put in its place. He went to all that trouble because it was already Thursday evening, and it would be impossible to reach all the signatories before Friday. We all appreciated his eagerness, particularly since we knew that his wife was due to give birth any moment, and that he was most concerned. The letter, which marked the birth-date of the ' Writers for Israel' group, was indeed published on June 4th. If my memory serves me well, Raphael's wife had a son on the 5th, and they called him Joshua.

I have gone into the details in view of the turn things were to take before very long, a twist which some regard as ironical, others as sad. We shall come back to this in the next chapter.

Meanwhile, events were developing apace. Parallel to the emergence of the writers' group, I had the good fortune to come into contact with a number of other writers, critics and scholars, who were worried also by the indifference of the policy- and opinion-makers of Britain in view of Israel's dangerous situation. This group met at the home of Professor Walter Laqueur, its distinguished participants including Leonard Schapira, M. Friedman, T. R. Fyvel, Leopold Labedz, John Gross and Dan Jacobson. With the voluntary assistance of some of these people—authorities in their fields —a publication entitled *The World and the Middle East* was mimeographed and sent out to a wide range of public figures. It was both a noble as well as an effective contribution, for it undertook to clarify the issues of the Arab-Israeli conflict without in any respect being influenced by official Israeli handouts. It was, in brief, a rare and momentous combination of profound Jewish involvement and intellectual integrity. Against the background of the rather unfriendly neutralism of the *Times*, the *Guardian* and television's news and current affairs departments, it answered a most urgent need.

It so happened that the letter to the *Sunday Times* appeared in print one day before the outbreak of the Six-Day War. On the 5th, a new letter was written at the initiative of Denis Norden. It read as follows:

   Israel is now fighting for survival. The openly

avowed intention of the Arab nations is Israel's complete extermination—nothing less than the annihilation of two and a half million men, women and children. General Dayan, Israel's Minister of Defence, has stated that he does not want British and American boys to die for Israel. This does not preclude our giving other forms of assistance. Our Prime Minister and all parties in Parliament have pledged Israel's right to live.

In the name of humanity, let us take positive and immediate action to fulfil this pledge.

We, the undersigned, affirm Israel's right to exist as a free, independent, democratic state.

The letter had seventy distinguished signatories, most of them non-Jews—writers, actors, directors, politicians, film celebrities—and was presented by a group of them at 10 Downing Street.

On the 7th it was published as a full-page advertisement in the *Daily Telegraph.* The *Daily Mirror* refused to accept it as a paid advertisement, and published it as a news item on page one.

On the same day, the 'Writers' Group' sent a cable to the Israel Writers' Association, which read:

We, the undersigned Jewish writers, wish to convey to the Israeli Writers' Association our own good wishes and those of the overwhelming majority of our fellow British writers. We know that many more messages of solidarity and support for your struggle for survival will be following this, and we have already voiced our heartfelt support for you over here. After our initial shock at the news of the war, we rejoiced to hear of your gallant stand and success, even though we do not underestimate the price you have had to pay. We are solidly behind you in your strivings for a just and lasting peace.

The letter was signed by all the Jewish writers already mentioned, and many more, thirty-six in all. One should mention A. Alvarez, Alexander Baron, Myrna Blumberg, David Daiches, Philip Levene, Harold Pinter, Mordecai Richler, Lionel Davidson among the additional signatories.

The whole atmosphere was totally different from the

one I had encountered up to that point and went far beyond anything I dared even hope for. I do not intend to write the story of those days, only to touch upon things which I was lucky enough to witness. For me it was one of the most meaningful events in my life, something that one experiences perhaps once in a lifetime, never twice.

Top Israeli actors cabled leading actors of the English theatre, asking them to sound their voice against those who seemed ready to abandon Israel to her fate. I shall never forget the morning when the phone in my office rang and I heard the choked voice of Dame Peggy Ashcroft. This magnificent artist had visited Israel and made many friends there. I had had the privilege of meeting her several times before. Later, she was to tell me how she had sat on the morning of June 5th in Brighton and cried at the news of the war. In the message she dictated over the phone, addressed to Yosef Yadin and the artists of the Habimah, Cameri and other theatres of Israel, she said:

> I send you my own heartfelt support in your heroic struggle in this war against extermination. I think of your country and the people I met and loved. I grieve for you all and admire you beyond words. I am sure that thousands of fellow artists are of the same mind and I know that messages of solidarity and support for your struggle for survival will be following mine and we have already voiced this publicly here. After the utter dismay of the news of war on Monday we rejoiced at the news of your victories, but do not under-estimate the price you have had to pay. Our heart and efforts are with you.

Many of her fellow-artists were of 'the same mind', it is true, yet I think I do no injustice to others when I say that active support was enlisted mainly through our fellow-Jews. Some of the Writers for Israel group, and in particular the indefatigable Wolf Mankowitz, had endless ideas of how to be of help to Israel. In those days Wolf turned into a one-man Embassy—phoning, urging, travelling all over town, planting ideas in people's minds.

One of these ideas was the 'Artists for Israel' group.

In a matter of days, famous entertainers were out there with the troops, from the Golan Heights to the Sinai Desert. Yet events moved so rapidly that before the scheme had entered into its full swing, the war was over.

Another somewhat bizarre enterprise, also initiated by Wolf Mankowitz, was the production of a documentary on Israel, not dealing with the war itself, but with the essence of the Jewish State as the home of a nation of refugees bent on creating a modern, just, highly productive society. I remember how the idea came into being one afternoon, at the Café Royal, where show business personalities crowded for an Emergency Appeal meeting. The speaker was Lord Goodman, Chairman of the Arts Council. It is a pity that his short speech was not recorded. I am unable to reconstruct it, and I would be surprised if Lord Goodman could. It was more the personal statement—I dare say, the confession— of a Jew who had been brought up in a Zionist home but had long since parted ways with his background, reaching a highly-respected position both in the legal profession and in public service. On that afternoon there spoke a man who fully realised what was at stake not only for that small country in the Middle East but for Jewish existence everywhere. Everybody present must have been moved if I, a hardened and sceptical Israeli, was so affected.

I had attended the meeting at the request of Wolf, and for a specific purpose. He wanted me to meet Harry Saltzman, producer of the James Bond films, and the director, John Schlesinger, who were both present. Like everybody else, the two of them had Jewish tears in their eyes, and offered their services there and then. Suffice to say that six days after the Six-Day War a crew headed by Schlesinger and Mankowitz flew to Israel—and it did not take much to persuade me, too, to join the crew and help them cut their way through the red tape.

And then it was all over. Those days were bigger than is recalled in Jewish memory—and they passed with the speed of light.

The sharp change from the sense of imminent catastrophe to total victory was more than most of us could digest, and left dumbfounded many of those who, just a few days earlier, had prepared themselves to mourn over Israel. The war was not even over when one began to hear the first criticisms of Israel. The pendulum had completed its swing and was now moving back from guilt-ridden sympathy to an attitude considered unthinkable after the holocaust. The Euro-Christians no longer had to atone for their sins against helpless Jews. The Israelis were the *victors* now. Their army was as 'efficient and ruthless as a surgeon's scalpel', wrote a rather friendly correspondent. Others liked to use the word 'blitz' in connection with Israel's army, and the compliment was even then a loaded one. Leaders in the press called for magnanimity and for Israel's unilateral retreat to the armistice lines, irrespective of whether the Arabs would agree to a peace settlement or not.

And just a few months later, in the Christmas issue of one of the Sunday papers, a noted journalist used Christian symbols in a way that could not but arouse deeply-set prejudices. The Israeli Military Governor's office in Jericho looked like that of the Romans in Capernaum, from which the disciple of Jesus had to receive permission to go to Jerusalem. The Israelis are the Romans. The Arabs are the Christians, or if you will, the Jews of Capernaum.

The days of May and June came and went with the speed of light.

We were left with the Jews, who had been shocked and had undergone a metamorphosis. There was not a single Jew in Britain who was not reborn as a Jew in those few weeks, wrote one of them, Barnet Litvinoff. They had discovered that their fate was tied to that of the 'eternal people,' that in the gas-chambers one kind of history had come to an end and that with the establishment of the State of Israel another kind of history had begun. So, almost every one 'was reborn as a Jew'. From now onwards one had to answer a different question—what kind of Jewishness was that? Did it really mean that they were not a living, Jewish people, or could it mean that the existing Jewish institutions did not answer the spiritual and intellectual needs of a lost, searching generation? Or maybe one should conclude that this 'rebirth' could survive only by means of a direct connection to Israel, by way of some emotional and intellectual 'hot line', without the various intermediaries?

This was, for instance, what seemed to happen to the Writers for Israel. The group came into being in a moment of grave danger, on an impulse. But it declined to dissemble. On the contrary, it looked for a cause. My personal experience with the group is—and will always remain—the finest memory of my two years in London. Having read Jewish history, I could not for a moment help thinking of Messianic movements which caught entire communities like bush-fire, changing them overnight. All these friends—and I do not exclude myself—were not their old selves any longer.

I have before me two open letters, one written in Tel Aviv on June 4th, 1967, by the Israeli novelist Aharon Megged, who was to succeed me in London, and a reply by Wolf Mankowitz, written on June 11th in London. Let me quote from the latter:

'... In the terrible moments when it seemed possible that Israel might not survive and that the Russo-Arab threat of elimination could be substantiated and Israel become one great and dreadful Massada, chagrin swept over us that we could not be there and fight and die beside you.

'For without Israel there is no Jewish people. From this time on those who want to remain Jews must intensify their links and their identification with Israel. The Jews must finally become one people....

'For my own part, I am 42, was born in this country, live by its grand and beautiful language and have always been a little confused about how Jewish I am....

'But as I sat this past Friday evening with a bare *minyan* in a small synagogue in a no-longer Jewish district of London to give thanks for your victory, I knew that these uncertainties had been finally resolved for me. In this small synagogue in which I prayed last when I was *barmitzvah*, I knew with pride and happiness that I, too, had returned with Moshe [Dayan] to the [Western] Wall—that today I am a Jew.'

This indeed was the mood of many. The group had meetings during the summer, deciding to 'maintain an effective organisation committed to Israel's survival.' But it did not stop at that. The members looked for ways to strengthen their personal involvement with Israel. Some thought of settling in Israel. Some took Hebrew courses. They were enthusiastically propagating the idea of an Israel Cultural Centre in London. Louis Marks, the honorary secretary of the Writers' Committee, gave expression to the general feeling when he wrote: 'Our continued existence since then [the June crisis] stems from a growing conviction among our members that the experiences of the war began a new stage in the relations between Israel and ourselves, and that the time is now ripe for this change to be given some permanent expression.'

Was the time ripe for change? Was it given some permanent expression? There is a Cabalist legend about a great mystic who used to go out with his disciples every Friday afternoon to the hills of Safad, all dressed in white, to welcome the Queen—the Sabbath. One Friday the Rabbi says to his followers, while they are thus standing on the hills: 'Messiah has come. Let's go to Jerusalem.' One of his followers, no less excited than the rest, cries out: 'Let me just take leave of my wife.' And the holy man—the 'Holy Lion' as he was nicknamed—says in profound sadness: 'Because of your hesitation we have missed our hour.'

Even before I went back home, about a year after those two unforgettable months, much of it was gone. The pendulum swung back. The story had no happy ending.

KING ARTHUR'S LAND'S END

EXPERIENCE HAS taught us that there is much to be said for finding out about things from books. After all, that is where anything of any importance is to be found. Yet there is still nothing like seeing things for oneself. It is common knowledge, for instance, that England and the Industrial Revolution are one and the same. None the less, one still needs to try and traverse London for oneself, from the north-west (where we lived) to its south-eastern tip, where the royal roads start out for Dover and the Channel. Then one begins to understand how the Industrial Revolution in fact gave rise to the hundred-headed, thousand-limbed, sprawling monster that is London.

One has to take a train to Liverpool and see what the nineteenth century erected there for the workers who poured in from the villages of England and Ireland—the crowded rows of black brick tenements, door-to-door, house-to-house, the 'stables of the working-class.' Then one begins to understand what it is all about.

One has to see London's railway stations, those dome-shaped organisms of iron that cleave the sombre sky above from the murky air below, giant cathedrals vaulting interminable platforms with trains pulling in and out incessantly ; the dozens of trains constantly pulling into Waterloo, while dozens of others just as constantly pull in and out of Victoria, Paddington, St. Pancras or Liverpool Street Stations ; the hundreds of undergrounds speeding incessantly along the entrails of the earth, ingesting and ejecting thousands of passengers at hundreds of stations strewn the length of Greater London—all the vast arteries of this so industrialised, or urbanised realm. Then one begins to understand what a revolution in transport really means.

When the time for migration comes, its wings begin to flutter, an atavistic restlessness turns its warm and secure nest into a nightmarish abode, haunted by questioning absolutes, by scepticism, warring values, by the fearless examination of truisms and sanctified values. One cannot escape the impression that the instinct of this migratory bird has the upper hand even in those supposedly warm and secure nests found on a New England campus, on the left bank of the Seine, in a mock-Tudor manor-house in Berkshire. . . .

The Six-Day War was over. John Schlesinger and Wolf Mankowitz went to Israel to make a film that would be 'with-it.' Many thousands of feet of film were shot all over the country and the crew was back. I was extremely fortunate in being asked to join them since I was thus able to see the Israel I had never witnessed before and will not, in all probability, ever see again: climbing in a small army bus to the Golan Heights, going for the first time since 1949 to Old Jerusalem and up to Mount Scopus (site of the original Hebrew University), standing in front of the Wailing Wall, where I was arrested by the British Palestine Police on the Day of Atonement, 1946, for joining in the final 'prayer' of the service and singing *Hatikva**. . . . And then we were all back, and the months passed, and the many thousands of feet of film shot in great excitement and under pressure of time were still struggling to become a message.

To make the film, Schlesinger had left *Far from the Madding Crowd* in the final stages of editing and must already have been preoccupied with his coming (Oscar-winning) production, *Midnight Cowboy*. As autumn moved in, one could sense the cold and dampness settling in the bones of all concerned. The scorching Israeli summer was far away. Where one had seen tears, there was now drizzle. Late in the year the film was finished, but I am afraid that nobody was happy with it, or what's worse, genuinely committed to it. One thought of a Message, but between June and November the Message of Israel had changed into The Recipe for Israel. Some said the film was too long, while others thought it too short. The media were satiated. Israel wasn't any more the Underdog of the Year—it had become

---

* *Hatikva* ('hope'): now the National Anthem of Israel.

the *bête noire* of the progressive intellectual of the Western world. It wasn't even very good for business any longer, and people weren't as keen as before to be openly associated with it. The film, christened *Israeli,* had a few private showings, and that was it.

The Jews of May and June, 1967, had become the starlings of November, 1967, the barn owls of May, 1968.

Much later, when finally home from my diplomatic adventure, I received *The Jewish Quarterly* (autumn, 1968), and read in it an article by Frederic Raphael, 'Have we always to be on the defensive?' The reader will recall those emotion-charged meetings of the Writers for Israel Group, the letter to the *Sunday Times,* the delegation to Number Ten, the child born in those days and named, how fittingly, Joshua.

And suddenly, the summer, after that article: 'I have never been to Israel. I intended to go there early in 1962 but I only got as far as Greece, where I became involved with a novel and where I bought a small piece of land, the first I ever owned.' So that his readers would get ' as honest a picture as possible of my relationship both with the Jewish community and with Zionism, Mr. Raphael points out that he was brought up 'in a part of London diametrically opposite to that in which the Jewish community flourished.' Various personal experiences led him, however, to realise that anti-semitism ' was a monstrous falsehood,' and like Sammy Davis Junior and other negroes who were trying to make their way back into a community from which they were happy to be free, ' so did I try to make positive what had always seemed negative features of my life. . . . *The Limits of Love* secured me an entrée (one, to be sure, which I scarcely solicited) into the Jewish community from which both my temperament and my circumstances had kept me at a distance. . . . From that time on it was assumed that I was "a Jewish writer" and because few people willingly forgo an amiable audience, I was disposed to allow myself to be lapped in so imprecise a guise.'

Then came the events of May, ' and I, like others, found myself swept along on a wave of apprehensive loyalty which quite exceeded anything I had expected of myself. The same thing happened to almost all the Jewish writers and intellectuals whom I knew. We were eager to do anything we could to avert what seemed like an imminent catastrophe and I would surely have been deeply offended had I not been asked to join the writers' committee on which I found myself.'

But the quoted article was written after the Paris events of 1968, and its purpose was to contrast 'two events which within the space of one year have carried a major personal and intellectual challenge.' In retrospect, the June war 'left intellectuals who supposed that they were about to see a civilisation destroyed feeling rather foolish. . . .'

As I write this chapter, more than three years after the Six-Day War, an uneasy ceasefire may still again develop into a full-scale war, and this time with the direct involvement of a super power. What ought to make one feel more foolish—fear of an imminent catastrophe, or the following thought and the rather unfortunate analogy? 'I am not at all sure that those writers and intellectuals who embraced the Israeli cause with such fervour did not allow themselves to be caught up in a situation not unlike that of naïve fellow-travellers supporting Stalinism.'

My experiences of those dark days of May will stay forever in my mind, and no retrospective musings will erase that 'wave of apprehensive loyalty' which swept us all towards one another. Still, how is one to evaluate the second thoughts of this sensitive Jewish writer: 'I would like to say, disagreeable as it may be, that in some sense the victory of Israel was both too easy and too complete for us to have an easy conscience.'

To the best of my knowledge, Frederic Raphael has still not managed to visit Israel. It might have done some good to his feeling that he had participated in the fortunes of the State of Israel only in 'the woolliest and most sentimental way.' He might even have discovered that this confession of an ex-fellow-traveller was a bit too early in the day. He assures his readers that his heart is still in the right place, but adds that 'on the other hand, of course, we also have heads.'

Using his head, he contrasts the Jewish intellectual's

attitude towards Israel with the challenge presented by the Student Revolt of May, 1968, ' to those of us who continue to lead a West European life which cannot be shirked.' More explicitly: 'The standards of the French students are of more consequence, it seems to me, to Jewish intellectuals and make more rigorous demands upon them than any adherence to the principle of loyalty to Israel.'

It may be argued that my quoting from that article is a little unfair to its author. The Revolt of May, 1968, has long ago shrunk into an operatic happening, while ' the posture of Israel as the underdog' is an even more unhappy phrase than when Mr. Raphael coined it. Let me admit, then, that it is precisely for this reason that I find the article so indicative of the Jewish intellectual's condition. For one brief month he was shocked into ' total ' identification, but the first turn of events frightened him out of it, his 'intellectual' Western self again taking possession of him and locking his ' sentimental ' Jewish self away in the dark cellar of the unconscious.

On a different level, but to me as indicative (and as painful, let me add), were the post-June utterances of yet another distinguished member of the Writers for Israel Committee, Dr. George Steiner. In a preceding chapter I mentioned that afternoon in May when Dr. Steiner phoned from Cambridge and in very moving words defined his—in fact, every Jew's—duty to stand by Israel in her grave hour, and not in words, but in deeds, namely by going to Israel and being of help wherever needed. The few meetings I was fortunate enough to have with him impressed me very strongly.

Again, the short English summer came to an end. The Writers' Committee still existed, and indeed a number of its members were meeting regularly, discussing ways and means of giving expression to their newly-found Jewish commitment to Israel. Some were trying to establish an Israel Centre in London. Some joined an audio-visual course in Hebrew. Some were seriously discussing immigration (one, Lionel Davidson, in fact took off and settled in Israel, without much ado). In real terms, the committee, and mostly its secretary, Louis Marks, tried to start a serious Israel-Diaspora dialogue by way of discussion groups and symposia, as an indication of what the envisaged centre would be about. As autumn changed into winter and the chilly winds of change showed distinct signs of heralding in a deep freeze, the committee arranged for a symposium on 'Jewish identity after June, 1967.' Lionel Davidson, John Gross, Wolf Mankowitz and George Steiner agreed to take part in the discussion, to be held at the National Book League, in London.

It so happened that a short time before the symposium was arranged I had visited Cambridge, as the guest of the department of linguistics. Mr. Trimm, my host, asked if there were other people I wished to see, and at my request he arranged for me to meet, among others, Dr. Steiner, whom I had not seen since the summer. Steiner and I had a very pleasant lunch at Churchill College and I enjoyed listening to his monologue (in his 'Rehovot lecture,' which I shall come to later on, he said, very rightly, that the Jews were not a people of dialogue). He spoke about his conflicting desires. He was very tempted by an offer to join the Hebrew University in Jerusalem, and seemed to be most unhappy with the English intellectuals, who (may the good Lord forgive me for repeating it) are by and large antisemitic. For his own and for his children's sake he should accept the generous offer from Jerusalem. On the other hand, though. . . .

Before going over to the other hand, I should mention that the collection of his brilliant essays, *Language and Silence,* had just been published in England, and when listening to him, I couldn't help but think of some of the reviews, especially the one in *Encounter* (December, 1967) by Anthony Burgess, entitled 'Steinerian Agony.' In the book Steiner argues (to quote Burgess), that there is an 'ultimate failure of language to provide an apparatus of adequate expression for the horrors of the contemporary world,' and that 'all that is left, after Auschwitz and Buchenwald, is silence.' His reviewer takes issue with him, especially on his attitude to the German language ('a language in which one can write a "Horst Wessel Lied" is ready to give hell a native tongue,' writes Steiner). Burgess, coating his criticism with words of respect and admiration, passes judgement:

'Dr. Steiner is a Jew, and it is as a Jew, not as a detached aesthete or philologist, that he reproaches language with its inability to cope with the reference that modern history submits to it.' Listening to him over lunch at Cambridge, I thought that I understood that 'scholarly man, with taste and capacity for suffering equally pitched to a hardly tolerable exquisiteness'—a man hits where it hurts most.

But on the other hand. . . . On the other hand was a reference to that fundamental question raised in the lecture he gave in Israel at Rehovot, in the summer of 1968, which was published later in the *Jewish Quarterly* under the title 'A View from Without.' On the other hand . . . is nothing less than the question of Israel's relevance to 'Jews who feel that the just condition of Jewry is one of creative exile, of provocation through radical irony and a refusal to "belong."' Steiner defines himself as a pessimist who believes that 'no nation-state will ever fully accept its Jews or keep its bargains of safeguard with them in times of political or economic crisis.' Moreover, 'someone like myself must do what he can, financially, by means of information and argument abroad, to support the State of Israel—knowing full well how little he contributes so long as he does not settle in Israel with his children.' But having said that, he questions this 'obsolescent model for economic, political and moral association,' the nation-state. As such, 'Israel looks like a solution which is, in part at least, irrelevant or even inimical to the criteria, to the obligations of Judaic humanism.'

Having read and re-read the published text a number of times, I cannot help discovering in it—albeit in new and exquisite form—the long-forgotten theories of the German-Jewish Reform of the nineteenth century. One could almost see the rabbi delivering a sermon from his pulpit in the Berlin or Vienna of the Enlightenment, long before Adolf Hitler was even born: 'To be wanderers and scattered among nations may, for some of us, be a moral necessity. . . . What have the kindred of Spinoza and Heine to do with flags or oaths of national fidelity? Yes, I am a wanderer, a luftmensch: "unto the elements be free" . . . I am a fellow-citizen of Trotsky and of Freud; a landsman of Kafka and Roman Jacobson; I need the same visa as Lévi-Strauss.'

So here we are. Raphael named his son, born in those June days—Joshua. A year later he thought the real challenge facing the intellectual was the Student Revolt in Paris. Steiner, in June, 1968, also remembers Joshua, the book, the story of the settlement of Canaan. He is driven no longer by the moral urge to participate, 'to sit in a pavement-café in Tel Aviv' so that he will be seen to identify. In the summer of 1968 he dwells on the ninth chapter of Joshua as well as on passages in Exodus, Deuteronomy and Judges, drawing a line to our generation, to racialism, apartheid, Nazi doctrines. 'Thus it may be that the Jew bears some part of the historical responsibility for the crime against man that is tribalism, chauvinism, the myth of racial election. That crime almost annihilated the Jewish people in this century, coming like a boomerang out of a travesty of the remote Judaic past.'

All this, however, was much later. Let us go back now to the scheduled symposium on 'Jewish Identity after the June War,' in the last weeks of 1967. A week or two before it was to take place, the Writers for Israel received a note of regret. Unfortunately, Dr. Steiner would be out of the country, participating (if my memory does not fail me) in an Anti-Vietnam-War convention in America. He was afraid he would not be back in time for the 'Jewish Identity' thing. When in the high skies, his heart will be with the symposium.

Louis Marks and myself wondered whether it was just a sudden change in time-table. The winds of change were cold and unmistakable. But since Dr. Steiner left a small opening, namely that he might be back in time, it was left at that. A day or two before the meeting at the National Book League, the secretary phoned Dr. Steiner's home to find out when he was expected back—but, lo and behold, from the other end it was Dr. Steiner himself who spoke. He explained that he had arrived back from the airport an hour or two earlier, had a bad cold and doubted whether he could come down to London and speak. We were, as the British would put it, 'rather surprised.' In plain Hebrew: I could not believe it. I waited an hour or two, and decided to try and persuade Dr. Steiner to make the effort. This time a feminine voice answered the telephone. It was my accent,

I imagine, that made the speaker, who identified herself as Mrs. Steiner, ask if I was Mr. Bartov. Then she added that her husband has just fallen asleep. I asked her to pass the Committee's request and again left it at that.

George Steiner never turned up. To the best of my knowledge this was the last contact the committee has had with him. I never met him again. Only after my return to Israel, in September, did I read the text of his lecture at Rehovot.

Why have I gone into these case-stories, and in such detail?

I do not really know. I can say only that those days of May and June seem to me to be ages away, that all the vivid memories I carry with me seem at times to be but a dream. Frederic Raphael complains in the quoted article that his name was appended to a telegram sent to Israel's Writers on June 7—'I have no memory of having given it.' George Steiner feels that 'there are in Judaism other perceptions, other politics outside this *polis*'; hence the temptation of Israel ought to be resisted. The Jew is the product of the Diaspora, ergo—to stay Jewish one should cultivate and preserve it. The world, which will never be a quiet home for the Jews, cannot afford to lose their genius. The Jew, who will never be at peace with his condition, cannot afford to trade it for Israel.

The case of the Jewish intellectual is to me—simplistic Israeli that I am—the same unresolved mystery as it had been before that short and warm summer. Or is it the sad old story of the Jew-bird? I wish to God, says my mother (and probably all the mothers of all the Jewish intellectuals), that we should never become dependent on them. But on the other hand, to quote Tevye the Milkman, we are in desperate need of one another. If we could have been one heart and one soul for two short months, why should it not happen again?

That summer a child came home from school and asked his mother: 'Are you Jewish?' 'Yes, my son,' replied the mother. 'And is father Jewish?' asked the child. 'Yes, my son,' said the mother. 'I am so happy,' said the child, 'because *I* am Jewish.'

TO: THE READER

FROM: THE AUTHOR

THE PURPOSE of my stay in England has come up several times in the course of this narrative, at times quite casually, at others in a rather more heavy-handed fashion. Now, in bringing this account to a close, I would like to address the last few pages to my blood-brother, the Counsellor for Cultural Affairs, in company with personages from the odd assortment of types he had occasion—and sometimes the great good fortune—to encounter from behind his enormous desk in London.

First of all, the desk itself. In all the forty years which preceded the aforementioned diplomatic mission, the writer of these lines had not had a desk to speak of. Either he had no desk at all, or he had one he would have felt well rid of. There was the time he joined a kibbutz, for instance, bringing a huge piece of office furniture along with him. The desk simply did not fit into his tiny little room, nor did it fit in with the egalitarian principles cherished by him as by the other members of his kibbutz. So his desk was handed over for use in the central office of the kibbutz, while a nice little item—the true beauty of which would be appreciated only in years to come—was built for his personal use by the kibbutz carpenter. He has long since left the kibbutz, he has changed flats and furniture more than once, yet he has never been able to bring himself to change his little kibbutz-desk for something of more than sentimental value. Upon arriving in London, our Counsellor discovered that the recent and radical change in his status was of little avail as far as the matter of desks was concerned. There are two distinct schools of diplomatic thought on the subject: some insist upon a huge desk enshrined in huge room, others find merit in a smaller desk placed modestly in a smaller room. Each of the two approaches has its own pros and cons. Our Counsellor, however, seems to have fallen victim to the classic resort of compromise: he landed up with a huge desk, which covered some 90 per cent of the floor space and at least half the volume of his room. Rumour has it that the room was built around the desk, under the quite reasonable assumption that once a desk is down, it will stay there for good.

So there I sit, locked between the wall and the said desk, my eyes straying out to the courtyard, to the trees rich in blossom, watching the hushed fall of the last few leaves, spying on birds flitting in and out, then wandering back to the mountains of paper eternally piled up upon my desk. There's a dreadful sameness about it all: papers come in, papers go out, but the mountains are there for ever. Each letter answered seems to breed ten more in its stead, like some monstrous gorgon. And I cannot complain. It is all divine retribution, penance for all the many letters I never wrote, the hundreds I never answered. Now my desk is daily visited with a pile of:

To: So and so
From: Such and such

and my desk in turn daily issues its own pile of:

To: Such and such
From: So and so.

In deference to the fundamental bureaucratic law of never letting a letter go unanswered even when it has no answer, I wrote more pointless letters in the space of those two years than I had in all the years before and more than I intend to in all the years to come.

The said letters were by no means confined to matters directly relevant to my job. The number of my well-wishers and bosom friends multiplied overnight. They simply could not resist the urge to despatch the most moving communications to me expressing all kinds of conceivable and inconceivable requests which a real friend could not possibly ignore. That in itself was well worth while. A man gets to know precisely how many friends, both old and new, he has.

The kind of letters I found most gratifying were those

that came with the request that I recommend a suitable girls' boarding school for their niece or daughter, book tickets for *Fiddler on the Roof,* get hold of a spare part for a particular kind of Japanese tape-recorder, track down a manuscript in the Bodleian Library at Oxford, acquire the rights to some off-beat play, evince interest in the invention of a South African obstetrician (guaranteed to double the I.Q. of the foetus), purchase a highly desirable new brand of hair-dye. The commonest plea of all was that I open my heart and door to the bearer of this letter, who is an absolute darling and could do with a guiding hand in the alien metropolis. I used to melt at the protestations of affection with which each such letter would open and then close, and I would hasten to reply in kind.

My letter-writing friends, however, cannot compare with those who actually took the trouble to come all the way to London to see me in person. Truth to confess, I still had memories of those not so far-off days when I myself would happen to drop in to visit an Embassy of ours somewhere far from home. I would blithely announce my arrival to an old friend, look forward to being greeted with a great show of feeling, confident that he would jump up, fall upon my neck, burst into tears of joy. Instead he would just sit there, eyes glazed with boredom, fingers toying impatiently with a scrap of paper, with the telephone incessantly summoning him to all kinds of important business. Eventually I would beat a humble retreat, take my leave in the apologetic tone of one who has wasted the precious time of an overburdened servant of the public. Now it was I who sat there behind a huge desk while unknown compatriots, who had never so much as noticed me in Tel Aviv, stared bewildered into my glassy eyes.

Let the reader make no mistake about it: London is probably the best place anywhere to spend a couple of years or so. It merely has two major disadvantages, beside which its many virtues pale. The first is that Israelis simply adore the place; they never miss a chance to visit London, to take in the theatre, do the rounds of a museum or two, have a spree at Marks & Spencer, be shocked at the exposed decadence of Soho. London's second fault is even worse:

its strategic position, as far as air travel is concerned. One's on the way to Paris, so why not stop off for a peek at London. One has some business in New York, might as well spend a couple days in London en route there and back—it's all on the same ticket. I soon came to understand what Galileo had meant when he cried out: ' Notwithstanding all that, revolve she will.' And my friends around her.

On the pain of the most hideous torture, I will not be forced into uttering a single word of disapprobation about public servants—though I realise full well that nothing I say against them will do them any harm. Do not expect, therefore, to hear any criticism from me against a certain educationist who, as an invitee of the British Council in Israel, came to conduct a tour-of-study without being able to understand, let alone pronounce, a single complete English sentence and who, on proceeding to Paris, spoke with nostalgia of London where, at least, he had been able to talk to people. . . . No, you'll hear no gossip from me. No detailed accounts of all those trips to and from the airport to welcome or take leave of visiting VIPs, the way one ushers the Sabbath in and out. Peace upon you, Angels of Service. Peace upon you in your coming and your going. You rendered me eligible for honorary membership of the Peace-Upon-You Movement.

No, whatever you threaten, not a word of complaint about the natural duties of a Cultural Attaché. Who, if not he, will accord a smiling welcome to the representatives of each and every institution of culture-art-literature-and-sport in Israel ; who guide them on a brief but thorough sightseeing tour of wondrous London ; who introduce them to at least some of the city's more famous sights ; invite them—pocket shrinking and heartaching—to at least one lunch ; take them to the theatre ; escort them to the ' Prospect of Whitby ' ; have a few Very Important People invited to a dinner in their honour. Who, I ask, is to do all this if not our very own Counsellor for Cultural Affairs ? And what, furthermore, is not an institution of culture-art-literature-and-sport in the Land of the Bible, home of the People of the Book ? And who, moreover, would be coming to see me if not a Very Important Person ? And suppose one does entertain some tiny doubt as to the visitor's importance, how can one snub a person who has just this minute been presented as one's very oldest, closest friend?

My wife, whose slender shoulders had to carry most of the burden of this overflow of friendship, used to say: 'It isn't the two years here that frighten me. After all, it's rather nice to see someone from home. They all supply us with at least one interesting piece of news and even when they don't have any inside information to offer, they're always good for some titbit of gossip. But what are we going to do when we get back home? I'm a working woman, you know.'

'Never fear,' I would console her. 'Even friendship has its bounds.'

So much for our precious compatriots. A different breed were the many inquiring natives who—in the normal as well as other course of events—would be directed to the office of the Cultural Attaché for Israel. It's hard to believe, and even harder to persuade others, that our tiny country with its narrow boundaries and boundless troubles should generate so much interest and regard. I recall a conversation with the head of an institute for educational research, a man well acquainted with Israel. You have there, he said to me in his deliberate, scholarly manner, the highest concentration of intelligence per square yard in the world. He must be exaggerating, I told myself. Yet I could not help thinking, if they all see us like that, mightn't there be something in it, after all?

That was how lots of people seemed to feel, at all events. They seemed to expect us to do things no one would expect of a far larger nation. It was certainly so after the Six-Day War, when people regarded us all as some species of demigods, but even before then things were not all that different. The Massada exhibition had a tremendous impact; it drew crowds of visitors, kindled the imagination of playwrights, composers, film-makers. And Topol, after that unforgettable opening night at Her Majesty's. London is used to first-rate actors and to big successes, but Topol was not just an actor who had made a hit; he was a legend, he achieved the impossible—in other words, he was an Israeli.

Take Massada, for instance. We Israelis are deeply

attached to all that Massada stands for, to the story of its heroic stand against the Roman legions for three long years, and above all to the dying words of Eleazar Ben Yair, the leader of the beleagured patriots: 'Better to die in freedom than to live in slavery.' Yet the story of Massada was not always so important. There were those who had read about it in Josephus's *The Jewish War,* but it had never been central to the Jewish ethos. It was only the new Jew of Zionist Palestine, the pioneer-poet-worker-fighter who rediscovered Massada. It took a poet, Itzhak Lamdan, a survivor of a pogrom in the Ukraine, author of the symbolistic poem *Massada.* It took a pioneer from Liverpool, Shmaria Guttman, who started an annual pilgrimage to the Judean Desert and to that barren rock. It took the new Jewish situation in Palestine to create the myth of Massada. The rest of the world took a long time to find out what it meant to us, yet today who has not heard the name of Massada?

Can there be any better proof than the excitement it aroused in the factories of illusion, the film industry? Every now and then someone would turn up, in person or through the offices of a common acquaintance, and announce in a confidential whisper that he was about to make a film on the subject. To his mind, it was one of the greatest epics of all times, he would declare. How was it possible that no one, but no one, had done anything with so unparalleled a human drama, worth its weight in gold. So we would sit there in one of the more expensive restaurants around Curzon Street —the prospective producer, the common acquaintance and myself—over an excellent lunch. I would be given to understand that the said producer had made his money in a highly imaginative fashion: he'd buy up unmarketable films, pad them with short strip-tease sequences that had nothing at all to do with the original, and emerge with a straight box-office miracle. That's the kind of miracle we're to witness, two thousand years too late, on the rock of Massada. Do you realise, says the excited producer, the difference between the pyramids and Massada? The former are monuments to tyranny, while here you have an eternal monument to the freedom of the human spirit. There's a rare combination with tremendous appeal—the historic conflict between Rome and

Jerusalem against the background of the stark desert wilderness, an intense human drama with a universal message. And don't you see how vividly the theme highlights the contemporary conflict between tiny Israel and her mighty foes ? I confess that I almost get carried away by his enthusiasm. ' Have you a synopsis or a script ? ' I ask. Of course he has, and a magnificent one, too—a story one step better than the original. How did the Romans finally succeed in penetrating the fortress ? Love, my friend, the blind love of Ben Yair's only daughter for a handsome Roman legionnaire. . . . I sadly finish my lunch, lend a listless ear as he spins out the plot of another grade B picture called *Massada*. A box-office miracle in the Judean Desert.

Or the earnest young intellectual who has made a name through one or two sophisticated documentaries. The Massada story appeals to him, too. He would like to do a film focused on the theme that all wars are futile, that no matter how lofty your ideals, how profound your faith, how total the sacrifice—it all ends up as pointless, senseless slaughter. He would be willing to offer his services if our government were willing to finance the enterprise. And he would use Israeli Army units as his cast. A very earnest young man with a sense of the macabre.

Yet another Massada project, one which I must admit I found particularly excruciating, was for an opera. One never knows, all these schemes might well join forces one day, and we'll have a musical entitled *Fidler on the Rock*.

There was no end to the flood of bright ideas—for films, operettas, piano concertos, pop-groups, prima ballerinas, the Last of the Just wanting to do some good for Israel. They covered a spectrum from the daughter of an erstwhile cantor anxious to have her deceased father's music performed in Israel, to an Indian physician offering the services of himself and fellow-doctors to go and perform a couple of operations in Israel, just the way they do in other under-developed areas. His services are not needed, of course, but who can refuse his good will ? Who can refuse anyone, who can extend invitations to everyone ? How does one learn to sift them out—the truly valuable, the embassy-fly, the crackpot ?

I learned caution, in due course. Experience was an

its own. I noticed the shabby leather bag he clutched in his long, yellowish fingers, the yellow in the whites of his eyes. No, he was not the man my friend had spoken of. To me, he looked like a northern autumn, black trees shedding their withered leaves.

I took him, as arranged, to lunch at the Fu Tong just across the road (oh, those restaurants that filled my stomach and emptied my pocket!). He proved to be a fascinating raconteur, telling story after story, and relishing the Chinese dishes. And I, realising I had got into something I was better out of, did not press the point. He reached it in his own time, after the spare-ribs, the sweet and sour, all the chops and chows. His long, veined fingers opened up the creased leather briefcase and extracted a portfolio of newspaper clippings, neatly filed in cellophane. Records of his great successes—in the late 'forties right after the war, in liberated Germany, in Paris, with the Allies. Here he is on the faded pages, young and handsome in officer's dress and tails, baton in hand and a world of glory ahead of him.

And then ? Then what ?

Then came the turn of the depressing stories of intrigue, malice, racial prejudice. He was as great as ever, but they would not give him a chance. Oh, yes, he still conducted. Witness this Cuban magazine and that Polish evening paper, and a by-line about the concert he had given in the Crimea.

And then ? I listen to his stories, wishing him a miracle that would wipe out the last twenty years, and pretend to be taken in by what his agent has in the offing for him. If he could only conduct in Israel, the country so close to his heart. I know that he would willingly take a job anywhere in the world, yet I somehow feel that he genuinely believes that Tel Aviv, more than any place on earth, will offer him the chance to regain his lost grandeur. In the dim light of the restaurant, the whites of his eyes reflect the pale Chinese tea we sip. I mumble something—true in itself—about the way that sort of thing is done in Israel, not through me, the Philharmonic would be outraged by such interference. It's the truth, but I can tell he has heard it all before. He looks what he is—a tired, beaten man. We rise and leave the place in silence. Even the impassive Chinese who helps him into

ON ONE INTELLECTUAL AND ON ANOTHER

IN MY bird-classifier I found very little to help me classify my fellow-intellectual Jew-bird, to borrow the title of Bernard Malamud's powerful story. The difficulty lies not in the rarity of that unique bird, but in its many and often contradictory traits and modes of behaviour. At times, it seems to belong to the migratory species, classified by ornithologists as cosmopolitan. 'Few birds (according to the *Britannica*) are cosmopolitan. As an example may be mentioned the sanderling (*Crocethia alba*), which at some season may be found along water almost anywhere on earth, but which nests only in the arctic regions, passing southward in migration throughout the world, to return in spring to its breeding area.'

Or should our intellectual Jew-bird be grouped with the barn owl (*Tyto species*)? As June of 1967 turned into July, and August gave way to September, I couldn't help but think so : 'Resident through wide areas in the temperate and tropical regions of the earth so that it reaches all the continents, it has reacted to its environment in such a way that more than 50 geographic forms, some sufficiently distinct to be called specific, have been recognised.' Isn't he exactly like the barn owl ? Hasn't he reacted easily to many climates, continents, régimes ? Who articulated the hidden national desires of Victorian Britain, of Gaullist France, of the Czech January Revolution, of contemporary America, of the New Left, of the Hippies, better than Disraeli, Aron Goldstucker, Kissinger, Alan Ginsberg. And Herzog, Portnoy, The Fixer, as well as their elder relative, the Salesman—weren't they symbols of the American human condition. Or were they ?

The bird adapts itself quickly, but is it ever settled ?

his coat shows a mite less deference to him than me. We stand on the pavement in the chilly grey afternoon he holding on to his leather bag, I trying my best to hide my feelings. He shakes hands gratefully, assures me that his agent will call tomorrow—and that's it. I never heard from him again.

And then another visitor, who claims to have discovered the Ten Lost Tribes of Israel. He is a tall, heavily-built man with nothing of the scholar about him; but he knows. They settled in the Fiji Islands? What makes him think so? Why, he's a native Fijian himself, so he ought to know. He has done a great deal of research on the subject, intends to write a book about it. What evidence have you? Well, says he, since the European missionaries came to the islands it is not so easy to find proof. But before the Christian conquest, they all had Hebrew names. His own grandfather, for instance, was called Moses, undoubtedly the name of a Hebrew. (My unspoken comment here is that the Hebrews call him Moshe, and Freud made much of the theory that Moses had been an Egyptian prince.) I inquire about my visitor's academic background and achievements. He explains that for the time being he is employed by an insurance agency, the trouble is that he has never been able to devote himself seriously to the Ten Lost Tribes. He feels sure that the universities of Israel are brimming with experts on the subject, which is why he is so very keen to be there. Had he looked at all the material there must be in this country on the topic, had he ever tried the British Museum? No, he has never been there, but now that I mention it, he will certainly take a look at the place. When he has a better idea of exactly what he plans to do in Jerusalem, he will come back to me. He never did.

They're all very alive in my memory, all the odd people who seemed to feel that the Cultural Attaché was just the man for them. I shall cherish them for a long time to come, and only wish I could give some account of each and every one of them. Yet, God forgive me, I'm not at all sure which of them might not be better off unmentioned.

I remember a visit to a college in the Midlands. It was all most interesting, and afterwards some of the students came to visit Israel and the idea was that some of their

Israeli counterparts would take a trip to England. Yet that was not what made the visit special for me. I had lunch there with the principal, quite a young man he was, an athletic type and extremely amiable. In the course of our conversation I must have mentioned the kibbutz I had lived in years before. His reaction came as a surprise. 'Which kibbutz was that?' he asked. 'Would the name mean anything to you?' I replied, half in jest. But as he insisted, I gave the name, and described where it was situated, about half-way between Tel Aviv and Haifa. 'No, I wouldn't know that part of the country,' he said. 'I used to visit Kfar Etzion and the other new settlements around the area not far from Hebron.' I was amazed. How? When? All of a sudden, I could see him as one of the British police officers who had peopled my childhood.

'No,' he said. 'I was with the airborne division. My company had the job of keeping the Jerusalem-Hebron road open. We were stationed there from, let me see, October, 1947, to April, 1948.'

It was an unlikely kind of reunion between two people who had never met before but who had a single stretch of road, and a very bloody one at that, in common. I had been back on the selfsame road, during those very months, escorting supply convoys, my illegal Sten-gun well tucked away —I had a handful of friends from the Hagana, ambushed just outside Bethlehem, knocking on the gates of the police fort there asking them to help us save the lives of the men stranded in two trucks which had broken down at the road blocks, begging for a long, critical half hour.

'I don't remember seeing you on that road,' I smiled.

'I was there all right,' he answered. 'A very young officer with a job to do, did not really know what it was all about in those days. Every now and then the Area Commander used to turn up and say, "You're doing a jolly good job, chaps. Keep it up." And that was it. By the way, there was a group of students, thirty-five or so, I believe, who had been sent as reinforcement and who were all massacred at dawn in an empty valley not far from Kfar Etzion. Do you remember?'

Who, in Israel, would not remember the 'Thirty-Five,'

not know who they were and how it happened? For the people of my generation, particularly, for the handful of students that we had been then, they had been very personal losses. Any one of us could have been one of them.

'Yes, I remember.'

'My unit did the reconnoitring and we were the ones to find them, stretched out in that long, narrow gorge. I never could get rid of the dreadful sight of their mutilated bodies.'

We were sitting over coffee in the college, in the winter of 1968, twenty years later almost to the day. A principal and an attaché with those few miles of road in common. We left it at that, and went on to talk about the future.

Who else? Who should I talk about before drawing to a close? Rather, whom have I the right to omit? For instance, that famed clown, Coco, O.B.E., who wanted to do something for Israel, how can I fail to mention him? His real name was, obviously, Poliakov, and he (naturally) descended from a circus family in Great Russia. He would like to contribute something to better road-safety habits in Israel. Do I speak Russian? asks Coco. I'm afraid I don't. Well, there is a saying in Russian, 'Feed a wolf to his heart's content, he will still long for the forest.' O Israel.

Or the elderly gentlemen who had been to Israel years before as young pioneers, living on bread and olives and anti-malaria pills. One of them is in textiles now, his home in the Midlands, his town house near Regent's Park, his summer villa on the French Riviera and his nostalgic heart—in Israel. Another had spent two years, almost half a century ago, on a kibbutz by the Sea of Galilee, worked on building the Tiberias-Zemach road. He has made a name in his profession since then, he is a psychiatrist, highly respected and financially well-to-do—but for forty-six long years he has been reliving that brief experience on the shores of Lake Kinneret. Yet another is a distinguished linguist: he has lived everywhere, but keeps gyrating about one place—Jerusalem.

On returning home, I take with me traces of a morning in Hampstead, in a rather sad-looking house, in the company of an intense, witty old lady named Cellina. Her father,

Nahum Sokolow, had for many years been one of the leaders of Zionism, its ambassador at large, a journalist and public speaker of note, for a time president of the Zionist Organisation. The two of us sit and chat in the high-ceilinged rooms, looking at old books, old photographs, old mementoes of Sokolow's trips around the world. In these rooms, I am told, one felt the breath of history, they were the scene of grand receptions, meeting-place of the Great. But now, young man, smiles Cellina, as she pours a last few drops of whisky into my glass, does anyone even *know* who Sokolow was ? Do all the so-called Zionists in this city know, remember, care about his memory ? As long as I am alive, everything will stay as it is here, as it used to be in those great days when the house was full of people, seething with activity, flooded with light. But afterwards, will anyone remember ? What about you, will *you* remember once you leave this house ?

I take with me the mercurial visage of a man who seems to know and be known by everybody, who in some unfathomable fashion manages to publish a literary journal, to travel non-stop, to get around and be around, always at the right time and in the right place, always mindful of the interests of his journal. To this day I haven't the foggiest notion how that journal of his ever gets published, nor by whom it is bought. . . .

I take with me an evening spent in the rooms of an Oxbridge don, an elderly bachelor, Professor of Classics. I remember the medieval gateway, arches, staircase, and the spacious room with books lying everywhere, a fireplace with real logs burning (not gas or electricity with the same kind of effect), and the old man standing at the hearth, bushy grey hair and pipe unlit in his mouth. His man appears from time to time, sets down another bottle of dry Spanish wine and silently retreats. When my host is not busy trying to light his pipe, or helping himself or me to a fresh glass of wine, he picks up the thread of his monologue of anecdotes, snips of gossip, gentle witticisms which pour forth profusely from a mind that seems to know nearly everything about almost anything. I see not only him before me. For a moment, he appears to me in the guise of some latter-day Faust or Mephistopheles, the ghost of some old don who has been living behind the thick college walls for the past five centuries or so. When I entered, my companion was a little tipsy and I completely sober; as I leave, I can hardly make it to the car—which I shall be driving in an ugly fog—while he is at his sparkling best, as clear-headed as any Faust or Mephistopheles.

I take with me an evening in the singular city of Bath, during the festival. Bath, which had its hey-days when the Romans had their Empire and, later, after Queen Anne started the vogue all the early Georges were to continue. Now—in the theatre, and earlier, in long summer dusk as well as later, at a reception attended by local nobility and distinguished townsmen—now it has about it the beautiful white, sad and muted air of lost glory of a Chechov play. Associations are an odd thing. Now, whenever I hear Chechov's name, I no longer think of interminable forests around Briansk seen from a train window on an early morning on my way to Moscow in the early 'sixties, I think of Bath. . . .

Our days on the island we learned to love, if not to understand, are numbered. We are anxious to be back home again, largely because of the events of 1967, but for other, more personal reasons, too. We take a great deal back with us, and we leave a part of ourselves—two crowded years—behind. We say goodbye to places and faces that have become dear to us, to people we shall miss, to the many young Israelis who are busy coming or going.

Yes, the circle has run full course, and we are back where we started. I see them come—young, tanned, charming, confident and awkward, talented, ambitious, determined to succeed. We have seen them before, in Los Angeles, New York and Paris. In England, as in every other place, they keep running away from one another and they keep seeking one another out. They long for the big world, the huge cities, and their hearts ache for that tiny country of theirs clamped between sea and desert, for the familiar, the warm, for things they can identify with. Many of them will return home quietly, like ourselves. But I can see the others, as well, torn in two, sentenced by themselves to eternal exile. One day, thirty or forty years from now, some of them may look back to the ever-vivid memory of days on the shores of the Kinneret or in the wastes of the Negev, like their older counterparts whom we mentioned before. One or two will be like Topol, youthful princes, victorious, admired, never losing that focal point, as basic as any instinct, their Israeli self.

I take back with me that opening-night of Topol's, the feeling we all had that his success had more to it than the emergence of a star. I thought not of Topol but of the Tuvyah he created, a far cry from the one Sholem Aleichem had in mind. Topol created a Tuvyah that had something of the immigrant Jew from Eastern Europe, blended with the Middle East flavour of the character he had evolved in the film of *Salakh Shabbati,* combined with the vigorous humour of an Israeli Army entertainer plus all those qualities we refer to—for want of any better term—as 'Israeli.'

It is time to stop, and I still do not know what it is that I meant to say. Put it this way:

Late one Friday afternoon, when everyone was supposed to have gone home, I was sitting at my desk writing. Writing yet another letter—

To: So and so

From: Such and such

Suddenly there is a call from the receptionist. Some young lady is downstairs, asking to see me urgently. In vain were all my protests, all my explanations about having stayed late just to snatch a few quiet hours to myself, that I'm fighting a losing battle against mountains of paper. Please, Hanoch, says the receptionist, the girl is already here, and you can't just not see her. This being a Jewish Embassy, and my heart being weak, the girl is shown in.

What can I do for you?

She informs me that she is an actress, has been on the stage, has just completed a film.

I apologise for not having met her before, for never having heard her name. What can I do for her?

Well, she imagines that I know that we have just had a Six-Day War, and that was why she had not been on time for the examination at RADA and they won't admit her now. Can I do something about it?

Did she really think it worked that way? Did she suppose my humble request would impress them more than her great charm and personality could do ? In other words—I see no way out. You'll have to take the examination at some later date.

Does that mean you're not going to, that you can't do anything about it ? The young lady was clearly shocked to the core.

I am dreadfully sorry, but a Cultural Attaché is not all that powerful.

If that's the case, said the young lady, what *does* a Cultural Attaché do, if anything at all ?

Well (though this is not what the Author said to the young lady, of course), he takes a clean sheet of paper and he writes:

To: The Reader
From: The Author